NECRONS

THEIR NUMBER IS LEGION, THEIR NAME IS DEATH

CONTENTS

THE NECRON LEGIONS...................................4
The Price of Power 6
The Awakening 8
The Necron Dynasties 10
The Awakening Empire................................ 12
Armies of Conquest 14
The Dynastic Legions 16
Overlords 18
Warriors 20
Immortals 22
Tomb Blades 24
Monoliths 25
Lychguard 26
Deathmarks 27
War Engines 28
Triarch Praetorians.................................... 30
Destroyers 32
Flayed Ones 33
Canoptek Swarms....................................... 34
The Sautekh Dynasty 36
Mephrit Dynasty.. 38
Nihilakh Dynasty....................................... 40
Ancient Empires Returned 42
A New Epoch Begins 44

THE IMMORTAL ARMIES...........................50

FORCES OF THE NECRONS........................62
Necron Decurion Detachment 62
Datasheets.. 64
Necrons Wargear List 65
Overlord 66
Lord 67
Cryptek 68
Destroyer Lord 69
Nemesor Zahndrekh.................................... 70
Vargard Obyron 71
Illuminor Szeras 72
Orikan the Diviner...................................... 73
Anrakyr the Traveller 74
Trazyn the Infinite 75
Catacomb Command Barge............................ 76
Warriors 77
Immortals 78
Lychguard.. 79

FORCES OF THE NECRONS (CONTINUED)
Deathmarks 80
Flayed Ones 81
Triarch Praetorians..................................... 82
Triarch Stalkers 83
C'tan Shard of the Nightbringer 84
C'tan Shard of the Deceiver 85
Night Scythe 86
Ghost Ark 87
Canoptek Wraiths 88
Canoptek Scarabs....................................... 89
Tomb Blades 90
Destroyers 91
Heavy Destroyers....................................... 92
Canoptek Spyders 93
Doom Scythe 94
Monolith 95
Annihilation Barge 96
Doomsday Ark... 97
Transcendent C'tan 98
Tesseract Vault 99
Obelisk.. 100
Imotekh the Stormlord 101
Reclamation Legion.................................... 102
Judicator Battalion 103
Destroyer Cult 104
Deathbringer Flight 105
Living Tomb 106
Annihilation Nexus..................................... 107
Canoptek Harvest 108
Royal Court 109

APPENDIX 112
Army Special Rules 112
Warlord Traits 112
Armoury of the Ancients 113
Ranged Weapons 113
Melee Weapons 115
Necron Vehicle Equipment 115
Technoarcana 116
Powers of the C'tan..................................... 117
Artefacts of the Aeons 118
Tactical Objectives 119
Profiles.. 120

PRODUCED BY THE GAMES WORKSHOP DESIGN STUDIO

Games Workshop Ltd, Willow Rd, Lenton, Nottingham, NG7 2WS
Printed by C&C, in China
games-workshop.com

THE NECRON LEGIONS

Long ago, the Necrons ruled the galaxy as its immortal overlords, before the march of time and the wounds of war forced them into hibernation. For millions of years their armies slumbered – endless ranks of deathless warriors held in stasis until the time when the Necrons would once again seek to dominate the stars. At long last, that time has come…

In the gathering twilight of the 41st Millennium, the Necrons are returning. Overlords and phaerons stride imperiously before silent ranks of death-masked warriors, their booming voices promising glorious battle in their long-forgotten tongue. Eldritch engines of war rise, propelled by arcing engines, while mechanical arachnids scuttle in their wake. World-ending weapons, the likes of which the galaxy has not seen for millions of years, stir to terrible life under the exacting attentions of Crypteks. Rank upon rank of skull-faced soldiers spill out from their tombs, like a tide of cold, hard steel. In their billions, the Necrons are rising up to reclaim what was once theirs, and the whole galaxy trembles at their coming.

The Necrons are a terror out of time, an ancient empire that existed millions of years before the Emperor forged the Imperium from Mankind's warring worlds. Once, they were mortal creatures of flesh known as the Necrontyr – a short-lived and quarrelsome race, whose constant wars of conquest brought them to the very brink of annihilation.

When faced with extinction, rather than fade meekly into oblivion the Necrontyr chose a devil's bargain, surrendering their souls to the godlike C'tan so they might live on forever. Thus were born the Necrons – a blight upon the galaxy that would spread out to conquer in the name of the C'tan. During this long-dead age, the Necrons fought what would become known to some as the War in Heaven, scouring planets and entire systems of life. The metallic march of their legions echoed across countless battlefields – continents were shattered and even whole stars consumed under the advance of their seemingly invincible armies. The Necrons' enemies fell in their untold billions before the relentless onslaught.

And yet, nothing endures forever. In time, even the greatest empires fracture and crumble. To stay the hand of entropy and escape the wrath of their gathering foes, the Necrons chose to enter an aeons-long slumber, reasoning that when they awoke the galaxy would once more be ripe for conquest. That time is now.

IMOTEKH THE STORMLORD

Imotekh stands at the head of the Sautekh Dynasty, greatest of the arisen Necron empires. A peerless warrior and pitiless leader, when Imotekh awoke to discover the Sautekh divided by infighting, he ruthlessly took control and named himself phaeron. Under his implacable command, his dynasty has reclaimed dozens of systems, and united many disparate Necron worlds under its glorious banner.

A skilled general and brilliant strategist, there are few warlords alive that can hope to match Imotekh's mastery of war. Tempered by the long years of conflict, the phaeron was already a gifted commander before he entered hibernation. The millennia have done nothing to dull his talents, and enemies learn to their cost that to face the Stormlord is to face their doom.

THE PRICE
OF POWER

Long before Mankind crawled from the primordial ooze, the Necrontyr waged war upon the galaxy. Born of a dying world, with bodies cursed by pitifully short life spans, they were a people bound by an obsession with death. Over millions of years the Necrontyr spread slowly across the void, their armies crushing those who resisted their advance while their kings sought immortality through grandiose tombs and glorious deeds. In this golden age of conflict, the living soldiers of the Necrontyr made war upon their enemies. But as their domain expanded, so too did the Necrontyr fracture in purpose and design. Thus began a series of brutal civil wars that would see the death of dynasties and the murder of kings. In their desperation to unite their people under a common cause, the phaerons started a war with the Old Ones, a powerful and enigmatic race that had long kept the secrets of immortality from the short-lived Necrontyr. This would become known as the War in Heaven, and the galaxy would burn for an age with its fury.

In their hubris the Necrontyr thought they could defeat the Old Ones and their allies, but though their empire was vast and their wonders many, the Necrontyr soon faced extinction. To save his people from the wrath of their foes, Szarekh, the Silent King of the Necrontyr, made a deal with the C'tan. Alien star gods of unimaginable power, the C'tan offered the Necrontyr an alliance against the Old Ones, and the secret of immortality. Though he knew such a powerful gift would have its price, Szarekh accepted. And so the Necrontyr became the Necrons, their flesh seared away in the furnaces of biotransference and replaced by living metal and cold, soulless purpose. Filled with renewed wrath and backed by the reality-sundering abilities of the C'tan, the Necrons rekindled their war upon the Old Ones. Worlds ran red with blood and cities crumbled to ash, and one by one the Old Ones' fortress worlds fell. Yet it was only in his hour of victory that Szarekh finally understood the true horror of what he had done. His people had been destroyed, replaced by a hollow race under the thrall of the C'tan. Desperate to atone, he betrayed his immortal allies, and turned his soldiers upon them while they gorged on the ruin of their defeated foes. So were the star gods in turn brought low, and though they could not truly be killed, Szarekh broke them into shards and imprisoned them within Tesseract Vaults, that their remaining power might serve the Necron cause as both an energy source and a weapon of dire potency.

The Necron legions had been decimated by the fury and carnage of the War in Heaven, while their treacherous war against the C'tan had seen billions of soldiers and war machines obliterated by the star gods' wrath. To preserve what remained of his empire, Szarekh decreed that his people would enter into hibernation. So it was that, as their remaining enemies gathered, the Necrons sealed themselves away within colossal stasis-crypts. Szarekh swore that when they awoke, the Necron Empire would rise once more.

THE AWAKENING

Like a whispered breath that grows into a raging storm, the Necrons are returning to the galaxy. Beneath the surface of countless worlds, their soulless armies stir within stasis-crypts. Meanwhile, cold-hearted Overlords raise their pitiless gaze to the stars, their minds turning once more to dreams of domination and war.

For sixty million years the Necrons have slumbered, their tomb worlds filled with dormant armies and inactive war machines. Now they are awakening as if from half-remembered nightmares, and the galaxy shudders at their return. From vast crypt-fortresses, burnished legions emerge into the dying light of the 41st Millennium, a steel sea rippling beneath the crackling energy discharge of esoteric battle engines. Cohorts of swarming metal scarabs, talon-limbed horrors and spectral assassins accompany them, their alien minds focussed on a single purpose – to reclaim the stars.

However, time has wounded the Necrons in ways their ancient enemies could not. What was once a galaxy-spanning network of dynasties under the watchful gaze of the Silent King is now a scattering of isolated domains. Entire tomb worlds have been lost – their star systems consumed by celestial catastrophe or plundered by younger races. Others have suffered technological failure – the cold hands of entropy destroying vital systems and dooming their inhabitants to an endless sleep. Even amongst those who have woken, the scars of time can be seen. This is no more evident than in the minds of the Overlords, who are often touched by madness. Their personalities warped and distorted by millennia of stasis, they pursue their own damaged agendas to the woe of all they encounter. Yet, despite the billions lost, billions more remain. These vast alien armies stand ready for war, determined to return the Necrons to their rightful place among the stars.

On countless worlds, legions of metallic warriors march forth from ancient vaults and into the cold light of dying suns. Races with the misfortune to have made their home upon these planets are annihilated in storms of gauss fire and particle beams, until only their smoking remains and the charred ruins of their cities remain. This is the fate of all who oppose the Necrons. In the eyes of the phaerons, the young races are merely the dust that has gathered between the cracks of their empire, and like dust, the Necrons will sweep them away.

Another strobing pulse of plasma fire tore across the Necron lines, ripping molten fragments from ranks of living metal warriors. Out in the azure haze, puppet-like wraithbone constructs and agile Eldar Guardians stalked toward the phalanx of Necron Warriors clustered around the flickering dolmen gate. Then, from out of the rippling portal, a Monolith tore into reality, its immense shadow falling across the advancing Eldar army. Filled with nothing but contempt for his enemies of old, Nemesor Orunakh emerged from the Monolith's eternity gate, green energy sparks dancing across his embellished war raiment. At his back came Immortals and fresh legions of Warriors from the Sautekh Dynasty.

In lockstep ranks, the Necrons advanced into the teeth of the Eldar gun line, their metallic bodies weathering the sporadic streams of monomolecular discs in a storm of sparks. All around the Overlord his warriors exchanged fire with the enemy, the whine of shuriken rounds a continuous high-pitched wail among the crack of gauss flayers as the two sides closed. But the Eldar were far from daunted by these new arrivals, their forces surging forward as they attacked with renewed fury. Vypers and jetbikes screamed out of the haze while a line of towering wraithbone walkers fired searing beams of plasma into the Necrons' metallic ranks, each blast and incandescent bolt sending ruined Warriors crashing to the ground.

With a flicker of thought Orunakh summoned the rest of his army, and in a tempest of crackling green lightning they burst into reality though the pulsing dolmen gate. More slab-sided Monoliths appeared from the curtain of light, their portals glowing with pale energies, while sickle shaped attack craft screamed down from the firmament, their weapons spitting death. Orunakh strode into the forward ranks of the Eldar, his warscythe hewing apart fragile mortal limbs in arcs of blood, while at his side his Lychguard hacked down any Eldar bold enough to dare to land a blow upon their Overlord.

Even in the face of Orunakh's implacable advance the Eldar held their ground. At this close range their weapons were proving deadly against the Necron Warriors, the constant rain of shurikens severing limbs and penetrating metal skulls. Before long, a field of fallen, sparking Necron remains carpeted the battlefield between Orunakh and his enemies. With a slow, dramatic gesture the Overlord unveiled a blazing emerald orb. Spidery bolts of lightning sprang out from the object, washing the scorched ground with green energy. Where the bolts struck fallen Necrons, metallic limbs knitted back together and battered Warriors rose to their feet. Before the onslaught of newly risen foes, the Eldar Guardians vanished under a wave of grasping silver claws and hollow-eyed skulls, their death screams drowned out by the march of a thousand metallic feet.

THE NECRON DYNASTIES

For millennia the Necron Dynasties ruled the galaxy under the dominion of the Silent King. Names such as Sautekh, Oroskh and Mephrit were synonymous with military prowess and political glory, hundreds of worlds prostrating themselves before the immense might of these dynasties' phaerons. Under the banners of their grand armies the dynasties held sway over vast stretches of the galaxy, ruling their people with an iron fist and crushing any who dared rise against them. Biotransference served only to extend this martial rule, until mental programming bound every member of a phaeron's domain to his will.

Time and the Great Sleep, however, have taken their inevitable toll upon the Necron Empire. Much has been lost. Once-great realms have crumbled. Dynasties such as Rythek, Horth and Astreon are all but forgotten, their crownworlds reduced to stellar dust and their armies little more than a fading memory of martial grandeur. However, these grave losses aside, hundreds of dynasties remain and many more are still locked in stasis. Those dynasties that have awoken now wage war amongst the stars, with ambitions to usher in a new age of Necron domination.

Principle among these is the Sautekh Dynasty, led by Imotekh the Stormlord. The Sautekh legions arose ready for war, and under the strategic mastery of Imotekh they have remorselessly carved themselves a new empire. It is Imotekh's will to unite his race and claim his rightful place among its rulers. The Sautekh, however, are far from the only dynasty to wax in power. In the galactic north the worlds of the Atun Dynasty, once a mighty power among the Necrontyr, stir to life. Within their stasis-crypts are terrible war engines and weapons – towering machines of mass destruction which the galaxy has not seen for millions of years. The Ogdobekh Dynasty, renowned for its Crypteks and their mastery of the arcane sciences, are building an empire wrought from solar cities and worlds of pure energy, while the Mephrit Dynasty seek to reclaim the world-ending engines that once slew the stars of their foes.

Not all the returned dynasties have endured the millennia so intact. The worlds of the Charnovokh Dynasty were scattered across the Eastern Fringe, and have suffered in the Imperium's ongoing wars against the Tyranids. The embittered survivors have formed new makeshift legions with which to terrorise the Imperium's colonies. Similarly, the Oroskh Dynasty was ravaged by the flayer virus, and many in its ranks have succumbed to the affliction. Now, when the armies of the Oroskh march to war, vast cohorts of Flayed Ones follow, draped in the skins of their enemies and steeped in the stench of death. Architects of their own outcast status, the Nekthyst Dynasty are widely regarded as traitors by the other dynasties for acts of betrayal during the Wars of Secession. They have, however, found unlikely allies in the younger races, much to the disdain of their kin.

THE AWAKENING EMPIRE

Scattered throughout the vast celestial wilderness slumbers the impossibly ancient empire of the Necrons. Ignorant of the armies that lie beneath their feet, the young races built their civilisations upon the tombs of the old. The Imperium, ever swift to consider itself the ruler of the galaxy, spread far and wide across the stars, unaware that there was another that had already laid claim to that title. Now, after millions of years locked in the timeless embrace of their stasis-crypts, the Necron Empire is stirring once more.

So far, but the barest fraction of Necron tomb worlds have roused to terrible life, but with every passing year the number grows. Each time a Necron planet is restored a cascade is triggered, and dozens more soon follow. Vast solar empires are carved anew from the burning civilisations and fallen armies of the Necrons' enemies. Piece by piece, the fragments of the dynastic domains are being drawn together, seditious Overlords and vengeful phaerons searing the stars clean for the return of their mighty kingdoms.

What the Imperium cannot know is that, should the Necrons ever fully wake and unite, they would face a foe as numerous as themselves. For now, the Imperium has had but a taste of the Necrons' might, and it is fortunate for Mankind that the Necrons remain divided by madness and conflicting agendas. However, these are but the first stumbling steps of a giant as it gathers pace, and even now powerful leaders like Anrakyr the Traveller, Imotekh the Stormlord and the Silent King are uniting their people under a common cause.

KEY

Crownworld

Reference Point

Active Tomb World

Dynastic Territories

Dormant Tomb World

HALO STARS

Scarus Sector

Calixis Sector

Finial Sector

Cypra

Kinbriar

THE EYE OF TERROR

Medusa (Iron Hands)

Cadia

ALTY

Belis C

Chinchare

Zapennec

SEGMENTU SOLAR

THOKT

SARNEKH

Voss

Terra & Mars

Meghoshta

Tamar

Xor

OGDOBEKH

SEGMENTUM PACIFICUS

Gatha

Nervkor

Ultima Macharia

Trantis the Raider's

Uhulis Sector

Craf Bie

Akator

Solstice

SEGMENTU TEMPESTU

Illustris

SEGMENTUM
OBSCURUS

Atun

GHOUL STARS

Icnarus

Naogeddon

Sarkon Dutonis Dimmamar

Oroskh

Novokh

Bone Kingdom
of Drazak

EMPIRE
OF THE
SEVERED

Gothic Sector

Goth

Draven

Dhol VI

Desperation

ian

Valhalla

Varsavia
(Silver Skulls)

Angelis

Well of Time

Nagathar

Qyrakotosh

Mephrit

Oruscar

Kardenath

Perdita

nris
Wolves)

Nephrekh

ULTIMA
SEGMENTUM

Thanatos and the
Celestial Orrery

Aryand

Molov

Gidrim

Avarris

Cocholus
(Daemon infested Tomb World)

Hexos

Triplex
Phall

Moebius
(The Twisted Catacomb)

Sautekh

The
Maelstrom

Nekthyst

Arrynmarok

Catachan
Ryza

Dark Maw
(Warp Storm)

Mandragora

Vengeance

Biogrod

Chogoris
(White Scars)

Cardrim
(Cleansed Tomb World)

Estaban
System

Dyvanakh

Ymga Monolith

Seidon
(Stasis Docks)

Zantragora

Trakonn

Rithcarin

Tallarn

Sarlok

Orrak

Hyrekh

Sekemtar

Medusa VII

Agdagath

Sautekh

Charadon
Sector

Charnovokh

Rynn's World
(Crimson Fists)

Craftworld Alaitoc

Macragge
(Ultramarines)

Reductus
Sector

Oruskh

Nephilim
Sector

Damnos

Bardic System

Tyr

Agrax

Gheden

Bakka

Antagonis

Nihilakh

HE VEILED
REGION

Salem

ROTEPK

Vorketh

The Black Planet

THE EASTERN FRINGE

ARMIES OF CONQUEST

The Necrons wage war as they did in times of old – their immortal phaerons casting their armies out into the great sea of stars to conquer the worlds of the unworthy. Armies of lockstep legions and contemptuous generals descend upon their foes, honouring their ancient oaths of fealty with the death of worlds and the blood of civilisations.

Aeons ago, the Necron Empire was a tapestry of interlocking dynasties that stretched across the stars. Each dynasty spread out around its crownworld like planets orbiting a sun, those close to the light of the phaeron's rule basking in his glory. The crownworld was the phaeron's seat of power, and the wealth of its vassal planets flowed toward it like an incoming tide. Secondary to the crownworld were the coreworlds, each one ruled by a Lord or Overlord of the phaeron, vying among themselves for the favour of their master. However, the further one travelled from the crownworld, the more weakly its influence could be felt. The outermost planets, known as fringe worlds, were mere colonies that knew little of their phaeron's beneficence.

Like the hierarchy of Necron planets, the armies of the tomb worlds are each beholden to their betters just as each noble is a part of his phaeron's empire. Similarly, the Necron courts form political webs centred around the regent of each tomb world. Crypteks create and maintain the Necrons' esoteric machinery, while the Triarch Praetorians take their place as enforcers for the Silent King. Under these, like the clawed limbs of the phaeron, are the twin arms of the Necron soldiery and his engines of war.

The master of a tomb world will rely upon his Warriors, Immortals and Tomb Blades to be the hard edge of his will, whereas Lychguard and Deathmarks are specialists used more sparingly, and only upon those considered worthy of their attentions. By contrast, potent machines of destruction such as the Monolith and Doomsday Ark are reserved for wars of annihilation or extreme enemy resistance, where their prodigious firepower can sweep away their foes in a blaze of matter-tearing energy.

Beneath a phaeron's teeming ranks of soldiery and forbidding techno-armoury are the auxiliaries – those more akin to allies than true warriors of the dynasty. Counted among these are the Destroyer Cults and Flayed One packs. Largely untrustworthy and often dangerously insane, Destroyers are tolerated only for the havoc they wreak in battle. Likewise, Flayed Ones are a curse that seems to follow the legions to war, regardless of whether they are called upon or not. Finally, below even these twisted misfits of the Necron Empire are the shackled shards of the C'tan. In spite of their world-splitting powers, it gives the phaerons great pleasure to know that the star gods are lesser in status than even the least of their slaves.

ANKH OF THE TRIARCH

All Necrons bear the mark of the Triarch, a brand upon their living metal skin that binds them to their race. The Triarch were a triumvirate of phaerons that ruled the Necrons, and the Silent King was the greatest of the three. In the 41st Millennium, the absence of the Silent King and the long years of the Great Sleep have transformed the Ankh of the Triarch into a reminder of faded glory. Some nobles still see it as the foundation of the Necron Empire, others merely as an echo of a long-dead age. However, the Ankh remains a symbol of the Necrons, and even those who have lost faith in its power still bear it on a cartouche adorning their torso. Each dynasty will vary the colours of the Ankh and cartouche to match those of their phaeron. However, despite these cosmetic alterations, the shape of the Ankh remains unchanged, each exacting curve and line perfectly reproduced upon the Necrons' chests.

Each dynasty also has its own glyphs, variations on the Ankh that identify its soldiers as part of a particular phaeron's armies. These symbols are sometimes worn alongside the Ankh of the Triarch, but are usually secondary in size and placement, mirroring the ancient relationship between the phaeron and the Triarch. Lesser soldiery rarely bear these dynastic symbols in full, as they are generally unworthy of such an honour; instead, elements of the dynastic glyph are used to identify individual phalanxes.

HIERARCHY OF THE TOMB WORLDS

SILENT KING

REGENT & ROYAL COURT
OVERLORDS
LORDS
CRYPTEKS

Each tomb world is ruled by a regent, who commands the lesser nobles of his Royal Court and their attendant legions and war engines.

THE ENFORCERS
TRIARCH PRAETORIANS
TRIARCH STALKERS

DYNASTIC LEGIONS
LYCHGUARD
IMMORTALS
WARRIORS
TOMB BLADES

WAR-CRYPTS
ANNIHILATION BARGES
DOOMSDAY ARKS
MONOLITHS
OBELISKS

DEATHMARK GUILDS
DEATHMARKS

CANOPTEK CONSTRUCTS
CANOPTEK WRAITHS
CANOPTEK SPYDERS
CANOPTEK SCARABS

FLAYED ONE PACKS
FLAYED ONES

DESTROYER CULTS
DESTROYER LORDS
DESTROYERS

THE ENSLAVED
C'TAN SHARDS
TRANSCENDENT C'TAN
TESSERACT VAULTS

THE DYNASTIC LEGIONS

The structure of the Necrons' legions mirrors the cold logic of their engrammic circuitry. Born of a rigid and regimented society, the phaerons impose their unyielding will upon their armies. Legions and cohorts follow the ancient traditions of the Necrontyr dynasties, and fight as they did when their warriors were flesh and blood.

The core of every tomb world's army is its legions, and at the cold heart of every legion are its Necron Warriors. Within the depths of an Overlord's war-crypts, rank upon rank of these deathless soldiers line up in motionless phalanxes, obediently awaiting their master's order to march to war. These are the currency with which the phaerons buy their victories in blood and fire, and the ancient nobility of the Necrons think no more of the lives of their Warriors than a Space Marine would the mass-reactive rounds in his bolter.

When an Overlord turns his gaze upon a world for reclamation or extinction, he will muster his legions. The war-hieroscripts of the Necrontyr instruct that their armies be fashioned around exacting numbers and formations. However, the legions are always in flux, populated with throngs of newly woken warriors or ranks of recently repaired soldiery. Thus, an Overlord seldom knows for sure how many warriors are in each of his legions, leaving such trivial details to his underlings and caring only that they march to war when he commands.

Immortal phalanxes are more regimented, as befits these favoured warriors. Often a lord will give his Immortal legions names to capture their grandeur, such as the Tireless Blade, the Unending Vengeance, or the Unyielding Harvest of Death. Immortals bear these titles in silence, as the task of killing their foes requires no words.

Doomsday Arks and other Necron engines of war are jealously guarded pieces of an Overlord's martial collection. When summoned from the war-crypts, their prodigious firepower is often the key to turning the tide of a battle. Those who do not fall before the unforgiving advance of the living metal legions will face obliteration at the hands of the Necrons' war machines.

In his arrogance, an Overlord will often lead his armies from the front, striding fearlessly into the fray to hack apart his enemies in personal combat. Even so, protecting their master remains his followers' prime motivation, and Lychguard will form tight ranks around their master, keeping the unworthy at bay.

RECLAMATION LEGION

Just as each tomb world is shaped by the lord who rules it, so too are the legions a reflection of the will of their masters. Entire legions of Warriors, Immortals or even Lychguard are not unheard of, but the Reclamation Legion remains one of the most adaptable and flexible formations, and is often the first force a newly awakened tomb world will assemble.

```
                        OVERLORD

      LYCHGUARD                      LYCHGUARD

      IMMORTALS                      IMMORTALS

      IMMORTALS                      IMMORTALS

       WARRIORS                       WARRIORS

       WARRIORS                       WARRIORS

       WARRIORS                       WARRIORS

       WARRIORS                       WARRIORS

  TOMB BLADES       TOMB BLADES       TOMB BLADES

                   MONOLITHS
```

When a tomb world goes to war, its ruler will instruct the nobles of his Royal Court to muster their legions in a great display of power. Depending on the regent's status, other forces may be available to him – battalions of Triarch Praetorians, the insane warriors of the Destroyer Cults, and the robotic tomb-constructs of the Canoptek Harvests. These combined armies are classified as decurions, and the Overlord in command granted the title of nemesor.

OVERLORDS

The Overlords of the Necrons lead the legions into the carnage of war, commanding absolute authority over their subordinates. Armed with crackling warscythes and potent weaponry of ancient design, they dispatch their foes in flares of blinding energy. Contemptuous of the lesser races, Overlords are utterly convinced of their own superiority, and act accordingly. Only those who prove themselves worthy, by showing courage and skill at arms, might earn a quick death. For all others, agony and humiliation await.

As befits their rank, the Necron royalty were given the finest bodies during biotransference. Whereas lesser Necrons had their minds dimmed and their personalities crushed beneath oppressive obedience protocols, the nobles' mental strength swelled. Unconstrained by the weakness of mortal flesh, there was at last no limit to their ambitions. However, the aeons of sleep have had unforeseen consequences upon the lords of the Necrons, and the unforgiving claws of time have rent at their psyches. Many have succumbed to madness, seeing the galaxy through a veil of insanity, though this makes them no less dangerous for their foes.

The various dynasties maintain a bewildering array of different ranks and titles but some terms are fairly consistent throughout the Necron Empire: the ruler of each tomb world is known as a regent, while nemesor is the title bestowed upon an overall battlefield commander, to whose will all Necron forces will be slaved.

Overlord Naszar, the Almighty Vengeance of Sekemtar, drove his voidblade deep into his foe. The creature snarled at him through fanged teeth, even as the shimmering edge of Naszar's sword ate away its flesh like water washing away sand. Tearing the voidblade free, the Overlord let the dead thing drop to his feet as he looked for a worthier foe. Then, from amongst the press of grey-armoured enemies, one appeared. Clad in the primitive ceramite shell of its kind, the newcomer charged toward Naszar, bellowing a challenge. Its scarred face contorted in rage, the warrior raised a crude-looking axe. With practised ease the Overlord parried his foe's first blow, ancient mechanical limbs pushing back against genetically enhanced muscle. In quick succession, the warrior rained down a dozen blows upon Naszar, the fury of his enemy's attacks pushing him back. For a fleeting moment the Overlord enjoyed the sensation of facing a true challenge, and somewhere deep within his mind he remembered the faint taste of fear that mortals feel when confronted with their own demise. However, like always, all too soon the glorious feeling slipped away. In its place there was only the yawning gulf where his soul might have been, and the same familiar malaise of boredom. Mastering his ennui, Naszar decapitated his foe with an expert backswing, sidestepping the vivid spray of gore that followed. As his foe collapsed, he looked out into the melee for another who might test his skills.

Regents and other high-ranking nobles often indicate their status through the use of gold in their Ankh of the Triarch.

DYNASTIC GLYPHS

It is the honour of Necron royalty, and a point of pride, that they may wear the symbols of their dynasty upon their embellished war raiment. Only nobles of the highest rank are permitted to bear their dynasty's glyph in its fullest form. Those of lesser rank bear only elements of the glyph, and the warriors of their legions are marked with even simpler derivations of the same designs. In contrast, war engines, such as Monoliths and Doomsday Arks, often display their dynasty's glyphs in full – they are considered to be the personal weaponry of a particular noble and therefore warrant a higher status than even the Necron Warriors that crew them.

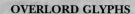

OVERLORD GLYPHS

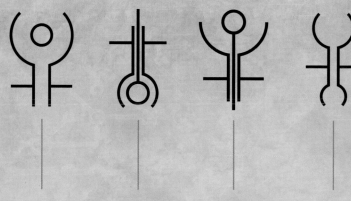

LORD GLYPHS

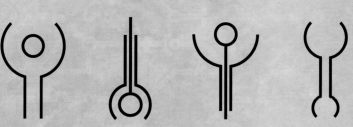

PHALANX GLYPHS

Units of lesser warriors and war machines amongst a legion are marked with a primary element of their dynasty's glyph. The simplicity of these markings speaks of their low status in the hierarchy of the Necrons. As these elements derive from the dynasty's symbol, the same glyphs will be used by legions from different tomb worlds within a dynasty, the legions' ownership indicted by the colours displayed in the Ankh of the Triarch.

WARRIORS

Marching across the smoking battlefields of the 41st Millennium in relentless metallic ranks, Necron Warriors are the unfeeling foot soldiers of the phaerons. Once, long ago, these were the common people of the Necrontyr. Their minds reduced to a shadow of consciousness, they have become the slave legions of the Overlords. Traded and branded like livestock, Necron Warriors are valued only for the destruction they can visit upon the foe. The phaerons coldly send them into battle to crush their enemies beneath an avalanche of living metal.

Even with only a glimmer of consciousness to guide it, a Necron Warrior is a fearsome and resilient foe. Armed with ancient energy weapons, they can scythe down their enemies with lethal volleys of gauss flayer fire, while their unyielding metal bodies repair themselves should they sustain damage. That the remains of the Necrontyr's mind, trapped in the Necrons Warrior's time-worn form, is only vaguely aware of the ebb and flow of battle, makes little difference to its foes as they are ground underfoot.

'WHAT CARE I THAT MY LEGIONS ARE FACELESS? IDENTITY MATTERS ONLY TO THOSE WHO HAVE THE ABILITY TO THINK: MY IMMORTALS AND LYCHGUARD PERHAPS; LORDS AND CRYPTEKS, CERTAINLY. FOR THE REMAINDER OF MY VASSALS? WELL, SUFFICE TO SAY THAT THE CONCEPT OF GLORY IS WASTED ON THE INGLORIOUS.'

- Imotekh the Stormlord
Phaeron of the Sautekh Dynasty

LEGION COLOURS

The living metal form of a Necron Warrior is a marvel of ancient science. It can bear myriad colours, textures and markings, and the Necron Warriors of two dynasties are seldom alike. Some appear as if forged from burnished silvered steel, their hard shells untarnished by age. Others appear as if cast from ceramics, stone or even glass, hinting at the strange technologies used to create them. Over these unyielding surfaces, the symbols and colours of the dynasties proudly proclaim the warriors' allegiance.

Necrons are haunted by the echoes of their proud, militaristic past, and consequently retain the pageantry of their once-great empire. Sautekh Warriors employ the cold silver and electric green used by their phaeron Imotekh, as the bearing of these colours has ever been regarded as the prerogative of the greatest leaders of the Necrontyr. By contrast, Nephrekh Warriors are golden-skinned, hinting at the dynasty's immense solar wealth. The Thokt favour the cold blue of their crownworld's immense void reefs, while the soldiery of the Hyrekh wear the crystal of their system's asteroids. Though the death of stars and the destruction of worlds has changed the celestial landscape of the Necron Empire, these fragments of its past live on.

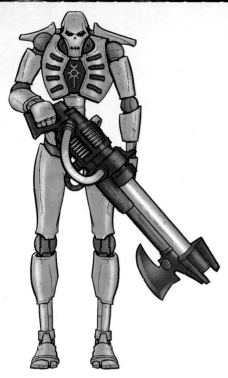

The ankh upon a Necron Warrior's chest binds it to the Triarch and shows that it has a place within the Necron Empire. However, it also acts as a mark of personal ownership. Legions bear the colours of their Lords and Overlords upon the ankh, with more ostentatious markings signifying a more important master.

Necron Warriors bear the colours of their dynasty and tomb world, and any other heraldry their Overlord sees fit to bestow upon them.

The use of gold in the ankh or cartouche is a mark of high honour afforded to the personal legions of a tomb world's ruler. The deep green shown on the right is commonly associated with the world of Gidrim.

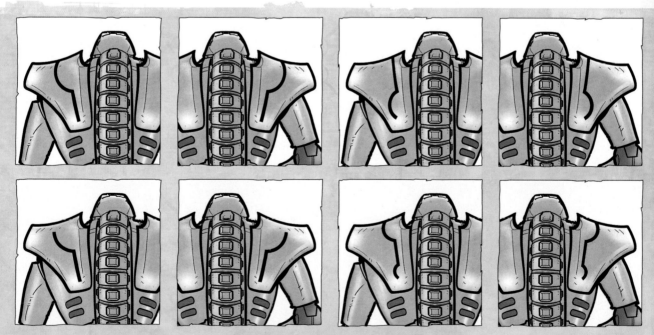

The phalanx glyphs shown on the Necron Warriors above are the traditional markings used to identify units within a legion. Each symbol is an element of the dynastic glyph, and thus legions from different tomb worlds may display the same phalanx glyphs. Particularly favoured legions may display their phalanx glyphs in distinctive colours that speak of the power of their masters, or commemorate especially famous victories.

IMMORTALS

Immortals march implacably toward their enemies, their guns unleashing a storm of gauss energy that flays the very flesh from their foes. Forged from the warrior caste of the Necrontyr, Immortals are the embodiment of the Necrons' dominance over the galaxy. During the War in Heaven, it was the Immortals that led the vanguard of the Necrons' armies. Now, millions of years later, they are once again assuming their place at the forefront of the Necrons' wars of galactic conquest. Bigger and more resilient than a Necron Warrior, Immortals can shrug off damage that would fell even one of the legendary Adeptus Astartes.

Within the engrammic circuitry of each Immortal there lingers a spark of the mortal soldier he once was. Though heavily suppressed by the obedience protocols of his master, an Immortal remembers the triumph of the kill and the pleasure of humbling its foes. The transition from mortal flesh to undying alien metal has only deepened the Immortals' hatred of their enemies. Stripped of weaknesses such as remorse and pity, and bereft of any fear of death, the soldier kills without hesitation. An Immortal's only desire is to enforce the will of his Overlord and reclaim the glory of the Necron Empire.

'WITH A DOZEN LEGIONS OF IMMORTALS AT MY COMMAND, I COULD HUMBLE THE STARS THEMSELVES. ONE WILL BE MORE THAN SUFFICIENT TO CRUSH YOUR PATHETIC WORLD.'

- Imotekh the Stormlord
Phaeron of the Sautekh Dynasty

Hyrsek felt only disdain for his foes as he dragged his mangled body toward them. One of his legs had been shorn away, the sparking stump scraping across the dusty ground behind him. In life, such a wound would have been a death sentence for the Necrontyr soldier, but now it was merely a momentary inconvenience and would not keep him from killing.

Crawling up over the edge of the enemy gun pit, Hyrsek reached out with cold metallic claws. A fleshy face contorted with fear greeted him. The creature fired its puny weapon point blank into Hyrsek, the las-blast leaving a glowing slash of superheated metal across the Immortal's forehead. Such feeble attacks were as nothing to the Immortal. Closing his claws around the mortal's neck Hyrsek squeezed until blood and meat flowed out between his fingers.

Flinging down the corpse, Hyrsek rose up to his feet – his leg had finally reformed beneath him, the living metal limb smooth and powerful once more. At that same moment three more enemies spilled into the gun pit, firing their weapons in panicked bursts as they charged. Rising up to his full, terrifying height, Hyrsek swung around his pulsing tesla carbine, the storm of lightning it unleashed illuminating his skull-like death mask as his foes were turned to ash.

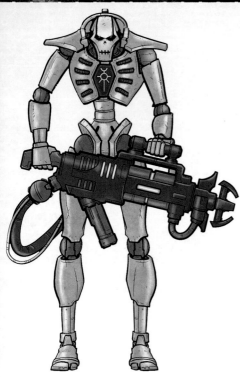

Immortals wear the Ankh of the Triarch with pride, their warrior minds recognising the symbol of their ancient empire. As with their lesser brethren, Immortals bear the colours of their Lord and Overlord upon their ankhs. These two Immortals display the marks of Overlord Zendrik and Azdrakh respectively.

Immortal phalanxes bear the same markings as Necron Warriors, though many also display an honorific band upon their brow to reflect their status.

A particularly favoured phalanx of Immortals might display the colours of their phaeron. This can either mean the soldiers are part of the phaeron's personal legion or are operating under the auspices of one of his most trusted Overlords.

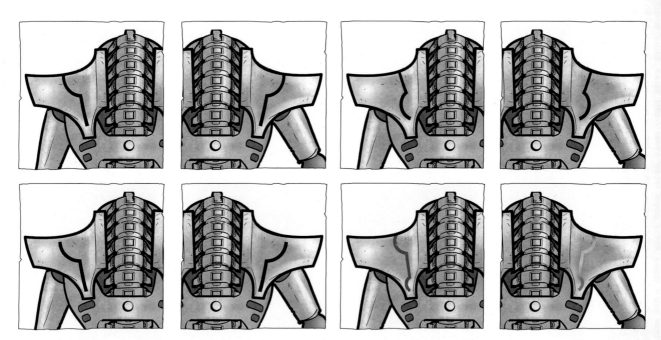

Immortals bear the same phalanx glyphs as other legion forces to identify them on the battlefield, which are derived from the dynastic glyph of their ruler. As favoured soldiers, individual phalanxes of Immortals may bear their markings in one of the dynastic colours as a reward for their accomplishments, or to proclaim the honour of their master.

TOMB BLADES

Operated by slaved Necron warriors but guided by super-complex navigation programs, these contra-gravity craft move with a speed and agility no living pilot could hope to match. Borne aloft by the ancient technologies of the Crypteks, the Tomb Blades were first created as deep void fighters, though time has proven them equally adept as operating in atmospheric conditions.

Tomb Blades are often utilised as scouts by the Necron armies, a role in which they excel, harassing enemy formations and descending upon lone units like mechanical carrion birds. Streaking ahead of the steady metallic march of the legions, Tomb Blades tumble and twist across the battlefield at break-neck speeds, seeking out new foes for their the legions to crush. Once a flight of these craft is set upon its task, it will not stop until its target is reduced to charred, smoking remains.

The upper struts and guide vanes of Tomb Blades often bear dynastic markings.

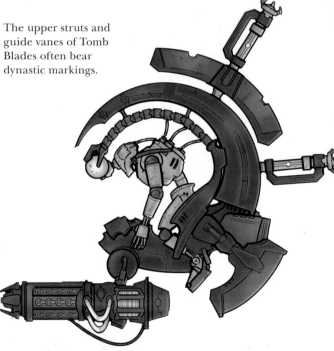

A Tomb Blade's pilot will display his allegiance in the colours of his chest ankh. Tomb Blades usually bear further icons and glyphs denoting their designated roles within their flight's attack pattern, which are applied to the living metal bodywork of their craft.

MONOLITHS

The Monolith is an ancient war monument of unimaginable destructive potential. When its massive silhouette looms over a battlefield, it will lay waste to entire armies with strobing torrents of gauss fire and the deafening crack of its particle whip.

Few armies can stand long before the immense firepower of the Monolith. Living troops are reduced to their component atoms by its punishing gauss flux arcs, while tanks rupture and explode in showers of molten steel as it focuses its energies upon them. By contrast, enemy ordnance has little effect on the shell of a Monolith. When damaged, the war machine's armour reflexively enacts self-repairs; sparking rents in its hull are sealed by living metal and impact craters smooth over as the reactive substance seeks to reassert its original form.

The true power of the Monolith, however, lies not in its in offensive capabilities or phenomenal endurance, but in the entrance to a captive wormhole that flickers at its core. This eternity gate links the Monolith to the vessels and tomb worlds of its dynasty – allowing reinforcements to appear at the Monolith's location almost instantaneously. Via these space-folding corridors, an Overlord can summon forth legion after legion of warriors from the very heart of his tomb world, with which to drown a world in its own dead.

The large flat panels of a Monolith's hull often display the dynastic glyphs of its owner, his personal glyphs appearing alongside other hieroglyphs.

A tomb world's war machines often display hieroglyphs in the Necron language. These may be battle honours, markings of ownership, or proclamations of the owner's power.

LYCHGUARD

An Overlord will grant his Lychguard the right to denote their status within the ranks of his bodyguard. The gold death mask shown here indicates that this Lychguard is the leader of its cohort.

Lychguard bearing golden decorations upon their ankh's cartouche are often the personal guards of regents or other high-ranking Necron nobles.

Marching in precise step with their Overlord, Lychguard are an impressive and terrible sight to behold upon the battlefield. Wielding lightning-tipped warscythes or spectral hyperphase swords, they exact a bloody toll from the Necrons' foes, their crackling blades carving through armour and flesh in welters of blood.

Appointed to serve as the eternal protectors of their Overlord, Lychguard tower over most mortal opponents. In battle, these imposing bodyguards remain in close proximity to their master, shielding him from the crude weapons of lesser foes. As befits their exalted status, they are gifted with more durable living metal bodies than the bulk of Necron soldiery, and their energised dispersion shields are able to turn power blade and plasma bolt with equal ease, making these elite Necrons even tougher to destroy.

As the favoured bodyguards of the Necron nobility, the engrammic protocols of Lychguard are substantially more advanced than those of Warriors or Immortals, and they are able to act autonomously if needed. Should their master decree it, they will fight from the front, guiding the legions in the absence of their lord.

Clad in royal regalia, Lychguard echo the grandeur of their lords. Golden head crests and segmented tabards make these warriors stand out from the common soldiery. Lychguard often wear the same colours and iconography as their master, so there can be no doubt as to their status.

DEATHMARKS

A single glowing eye distinguishes the Deathmark from other Necrons. Sometimes, Deathmarks will also bear faceplate colours that hark back to the Necrontyr assassination guilds of old. These markings identify the Deathmark as a warrior who fights outside the traditional code of war at the will of his phaeron.

Deathmarks may adopt the dynastic colours of their employer, although some bands of these assassins are known throughout the Necron Empire by their distinctive colours and markings.

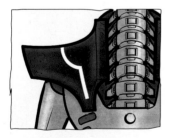

Deathmark units usually bear phalanx glyphs just as other units do, according to the dynasty they hail from. Sometimes, however, a phalanx may intentionally obscure their markings to aid their concealment on the battlefield.

It it not unusual for Deathmarks to fight alongside the legions of another tomb world or dynasty – though many nobles eschew the assassins' use, they are the not above entrusting them to an ally to further their own ends.

Crackling into reality in the middle of battle to annihilate their enemies, Deathmarks are the assassins of the Necron cohorts. These specialist killers are possessed of a patience known only to the undying, and once a Deathmark has marked its prey, nothing will stand between it and its target. Unerringly accurate and single-minded in their devotion to the kill, they are often employed to locate and destroy enemy commanders, or hunt down priority targets in order to disrupt their foe's strategy. Though some phaerons consider the use of the Deathmarks to contravene the ancient Necrontyr codes of honour, none can dispute their effectiveness when given a target.

Deathmarks have the terrifying ability to slip beyond realspace to pursue their quarry, ambushing from pocket dimensions detached from the material universe. From these timeless places they dispassionately analyse the flow of battle, awaiting the perfect moment to flicker into reality and strike. Physical defences offer no sanctuary against a squad of Deathmarks: towering ramparts, subterranean bunkers and vast gateways are bypassed as though no barrier existed at all. Few are they who have fallen beneath the crosshairs of a Deathmark's synaptic disintegrator and lived to know of it.

WAR ENGINES

War unending has driven the Necrons to develop myriad engines of destruction, and through them they have perfected the art of invasion and terror tactics. Night Scythes scream down from the skies in the vanguard of their armies, the sickle-shaped craft scorching the enemy with attack runs of lashing tesla fire. As a forerunner of an incursion, the Night Scythe is agile enough to slip past planetary defences, while a speculum affixed to the underside of its hull projects a wormhole gateway, allowing troops to be delivered directly into battle.

In their wake, supersonic Doom Scythes scour the skies of enemy aircraft, opening the way for a full-scale invasion. These craft are armed with terrifying death rays – energy weapons of incredible potency that can carve through even the thickest armour with horrifying ease.

Gliding over the battlefield, Annihilation Barges specialise in obliterating infantry, their twin tesla destructors ripping apart enemy formations in storms of arcing energy discharge. Living tissue is especially vulnerable to the guns housed by these weapon platforms, as flesh cooks under the extreme currents forced through it.

LIVING METAL

The war machines of the Necrons are things of impossible science and countless arcane technologies. To the young races of the galaxy, the energies and weaponry of these strange engines of destruction are more akin to magic than anything recognisable as physical engineering. Living metal is a perfect example of this kind of advanced technology – a substance that defies harm by literally healing itself before the eyes of its attacker. Though the means can vary between dynasties and the skills of the Crypteks that serve them, this miracle is often the result of billions-strong swarms of nanoscarabs crawling under the skin of the war machine. Like the living cells of biological creatures they will seek out damaged areas and cluster around them, mouths the size of atoms chewing up matter and forging it back together.

However, as with most of the Necrons' arcane techno-sciences, there are almost as many ways to manipulate matter as there are Crypteks. Captive phase-gates, subatomic infusers and temporal loop shrouds can all exhibit similar effects to nanoscarab swarms. To an Overlord, how these abilities work are of little concern, as long as they do.

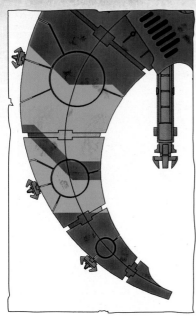

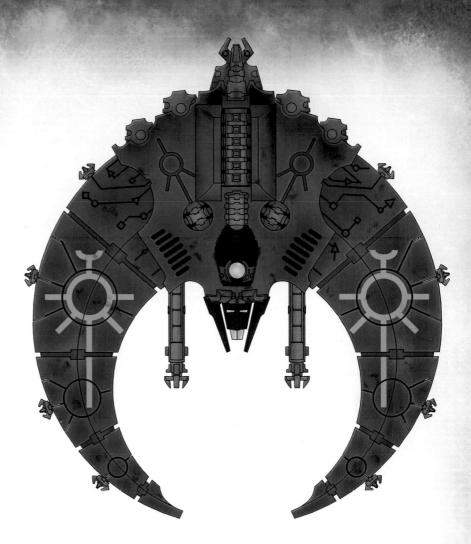

War engines grouped together to form a battlefield formation, such as a Doom Scythe Deathbringer flight, are often marked with simple glyphs upon the living metal superstructure of their vehicles to show their role within the formation.

War engines and their crew display the dynastic colours of their master in the Ankh of the Triarch, demonstrating the dominion of their liege to all who bear witness to them on the battlefield.

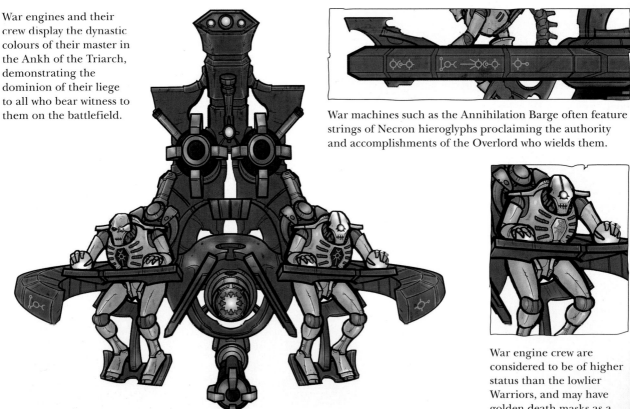

War machines such as the Annihilation Barge often feature strings of Necron hieroglyphs proclaiming the authority and accomplishments of the Overlord who wields them.

War engine crew are considered to be of higher status than the lowlier Warriors, and may have golden death masks as a sign of their station.

TRIARCH PRAETORIANS

Praetorians are the will of the Triarch made manifest. When the Necrons entered their long slumber, the Praetorians remained awake to preserve what little remained of the Silent King's empire. Bound to protect the dynasties, they have awaited the time when the Necron race might once again force the stars to bow before them. Now, that time is finally at hand, and the Praetorians seek out stirring tomb worlds to guide and protect their Necron inhabitants during the reawakening process. Even with minds affected by the Great Sleep, most phaerons still recognise the authority of the Triarch, and will treat with the Praetorians accordingly. When at war, Praetorians hover over the battle on gravity displacement packs before striking where their intervention will have the greatest impact, reducing foes to ash with their rods of covenant.

The Triarch Stalkers that often accompany them are frighteningly agile machines for their size, skittering with ease over terrain that would prove hazardous to the walkers of other races. Their Praetorian pilots can modulate the Stalker's heat ray to reduce enemy armour to molten slag, or incinerate swathes of infantry.

'LET ME TELL YOU OF MY FUTURE. MY HAND WILL REACH OUT INTO THE STARS, RESHAPING THE GALAXY INTO A PLACE OF ORDER AND UNITY. UNDER MY REIGN, THE KINGDOMS OF OLD SHALL LIVE AGAIN, REBORN TO AN AGE OF POWER AND GLORY THE LIKE OF WHICH YOU CAN ONLY IMAGINE. I WILL RULE EVERY PLANET TOUCHED BY THE LIGHT OF THIS STAR AND, EVEN IN THE DARKNESS BEYOND, MY NAME WILL BE WHISPERED WITH FEAR AND RESPECT.'

- *Imotekh the Stormlord to Eldorath Starbane,
in the wake of the Siege of Somonor*

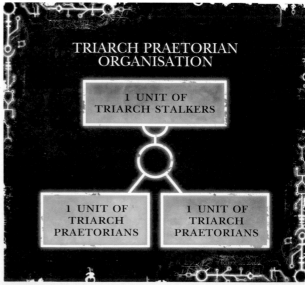

TRIARCH PRAETORIAN ORGANISATION

1 UNIT OF TRIARCH STALKERS

1 UNIT OF TRIARCH PRAETORIANS

1 UNIT OF TRIARCH PRAETORIANS

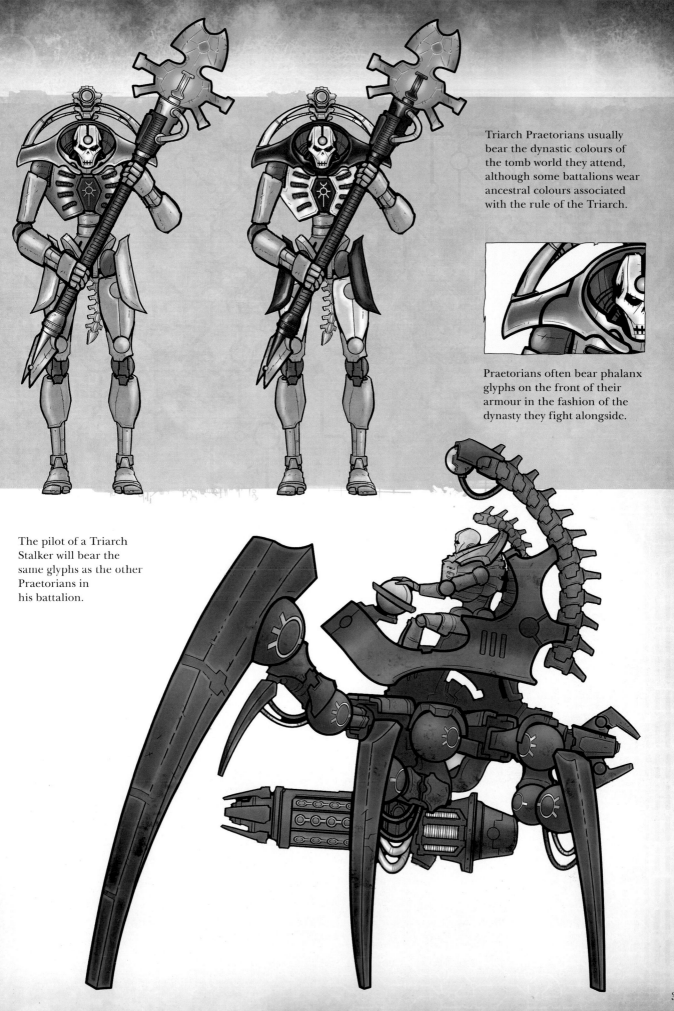

Triarch Praetorians usually bear the dynastic colours of the tomb world they attend, although some battalions wear ancestral colours associated with the rule of the Triarch.

Praetorians often bear phalanx glyphs on the front of their armour in the fashion of the dynasty they fight alongside.

The pilot of a Triarch Stalker will bear the same glyphs as the other Praetorians in his battalion.

DESTROYERS

Destroyers are consumed by a hatred of all life. Any shreds of their souls that might have survived biotransference have been scoured away by the Great Sleep. Even among the pitiless ranks of the dynasties, the Destroyers are considered violent and excessive in the methods they employ to war they wage upon the living. However, most phaerons are loath to squander a weapon, especially one as effective as a Destroyer Cult.

Destroyers scythe down their enemies with relentless salvos of gauss fire, while those who flee or foolishly try to surrender are mercilessly eradicated. Overlords have only limited control over the actions of a Destroyer Cult, and close to none when battle has been joined. Once a Destroyer has its prey in sight it gives no thought to the directives of its superiors, nor to the tactical nuances of combat – only the need to obliterate the living drives it onward, until there is nothing left to kill.

Their minds riddled with the nihilistic madness that permeates the cults, Destroyers willingly abandon any vestiges of their mortal selves so that they might more efficiently reap a bloody harvest. Legs are shorn away in favour of suspensor platforms, while heavy energy cannons are grafted in the place of arms. In the end, all that remains is a living metal shell perfectly fashioned for the single purpose of scouring the galaxy clean of life.

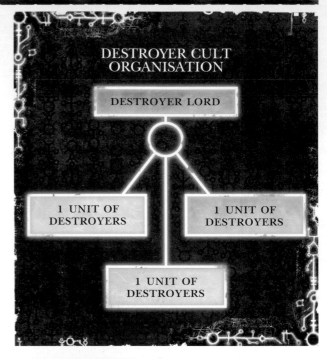

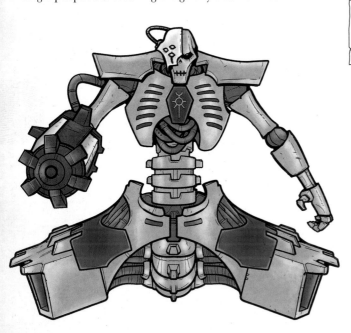

Destroyers commonly bear the dynastic colours of their home tomb world and its ruler, although some Destroyer Cults and their lords have grown so powerful that their own colours and markings are as famous as those of any awakened dynasty.

FLAYED ONES

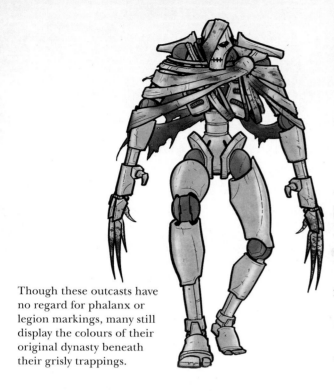

Though these outcasts have no regard for phalanx or legion markings, many still display the colours of their original dynasty beneath their grisly trappings.

Flayed ones drape themselves in the flesh of their victims, their obsession leading them to maintain a layer of freshly flayed skin.

Draped in the torn, dripping skins of their victims, the Flayed Ones creep through the shadows. Their ghastly appearance can be attributed to the flayer virus – a curse of the C'tan Llandu'gor. Cast upon his betrayers in his final moments of existence, it has ravaged the minds of certain doomed Necrons, awakening in them an unquenchable hunger for the warm flesh and blood of the living. Though it can gain no sustenance from its prey, a Flayed One still uselessly crams gobbets of meat into its mouth, runnels of gore running like crimson rivers between the grille of its metal ribcage.

Those afflicted are banished from their tomb worlds, lest their curse spread further. Some lords have even attempted to exterminate the Flayed Ones in order to bring an end to their malady – so far, however, these efforts have been in vain. By instinct, the outcast Flayed Ones gather in the Bone Kingdom of Drazak, drawn together by the stench of rotting meat and dried blood. Though they heed no master, when the legions march to war Flayed Ones will often wriggle through the skin of reality to follow. Then, when the scent of death is thick upon the air and the screams of the dying echo across the battlefield, they will strike, long, needle-like claws carving apart their foes in a frenzy of blood and carnage.

CANOPTEK SWARMS

Within the shadowy depths of Necron tomb worlds, billions of mechanical constructs crawl within the darkness. These are the Canoptek swarms – relentless robotic workers created for the eternal task of keeping the stasis-crypts functioning, and preparing for their immortal masters' return. While the Necrons slumber, these insect-like creatures crawl and scuttle across the complex inner workings of the tomb according to their world's master program, ready to repel any that would dare trespass within their silent halls.

When a regent rouses his world to war, the Canoptek swarms do not forget their duties of defence. Wraiths dart across the ground like metallic apparitions, their destabilisation matrices enabling them to phase in and out of reality to avoid enemy fire. The same esoteric technologies that allow the Wraith to slip out of sync with realspace also allow it to tear apart an enemy from the inside – the construct's claws simply enter the space occupied by their target before suddenly becoming solid. The attack violently displaces their foe's internal organs in a burst of gore, and even as the Wraith ghosts away, the lifeless remains of its victim fall mangled to the ground.

Equipped with gravity-displacement engines, Canoptek Spyders glide above the battlefield like massive arachnids crawling across invisible webs. Their complex programming allow them to restore damaged Necron machinery, be it the arcane workings of a stasis crypt or the living metal shell of a Monolith. Spyders also possess the ability to rapidly manufacture swarms of diminutive drone-like constructs in vast, shimmering clouds. These Canoptek Scarabs envelop organic and inorganic structures alike, their entropic mandibles breaking down even the most durable substances into stored energy that the Necrons use as fuel for the legions.

CANOPTEK SWARM ORGANISATION

1 UNIT OF
CANOPTEK SPYDERS

1 UNIT OF
CANOPTEK
SCARABS

1 UNIT OF
CANOPTEK
WRAITHS

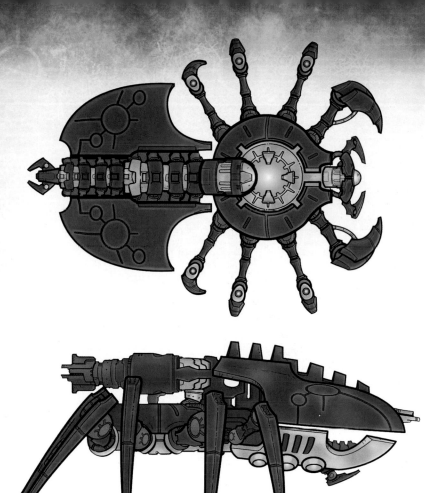

Constructs within a Canoptek Swarm may be marked with hieroglyphs that bind them together. The glyphs pictured here display the identifying symbols of the Crypteks who maintain them.

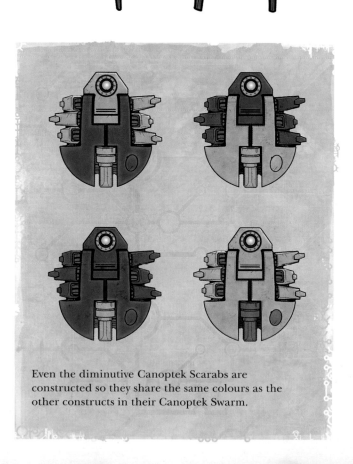

Even the diminutive Canoptek Scarabs are constructed so they share the same colours as the other constructs in their Canoptek Swarm.

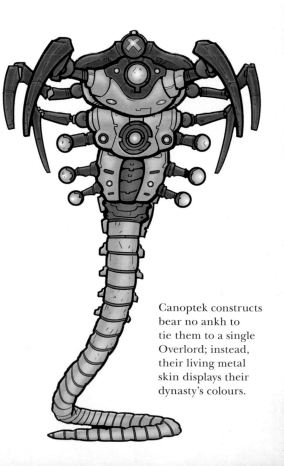

Canoptek constructs bear no ankh to tie them to a single Overlord; instead, their living metal skin displays their dynasty's colours.

THE SAUTEKH DYNASTY

Like a steel claw bursting from the heart of the galaxy, the Sautekh Dynasty emerged from the Great Sleep in a storm of death and destruction. Unified under the iron will of Imotekh the Stormlord, the Sautekh wield a power and purpose like no other dynasty. From their crownworld of Mandragora, the implacable legions of Imotekh spread out across the stars, bringing more and more worlds under the rule of their phaeron. Even other Necron dynasties bow down to the power of the Sautekh, joining the ranks of the resurgent empire. Overlord Naszar of the Sekemtar, and Overlord Szaron of the Arrynmarok have both pledged themselves to Imotekh's cause, hungry for a piece of the domain he is carving from the stars.

Resplendent in burnished silver and cold emerald, the legions of the Sautekh have brought to heel scores of worlds across the Eastern Fringe. By the light of burning civilisations, Imotekh's armies march relentlessly on, driven by the Stormlord's dreams of conquest and reunification. It is Imotekh's will that his people be forged anew, and that he rise to rule all Necrons. At first, the phaeron's desire was born of necessity, as he awoke to find his tomb world wracked by infighting. Rather than pick sides, the Stormlord dispatched his rivals and seized power for himself. Now, as the influence of the Sautekh waxes, so too does that of Imotekh, and the former nemesor sees himself as the architect of the Necrons' return to primacy.

As the most numerous of the arisen Necron dynasties, it is the Sautekh that have been encountered most frequently by other races. To the Imperium, the dynasty has become synonymous with the Necrons, and it is erroneously believed by many that they represent the alien race as a whole, with all other dynasties being mere offshoots of the Sautekh. The Tau see the dynasty as representatives of an emergent power, and seek as ever to form allegiances before resorting to all-out war. To the Eldar, the Stormlord represents the greatest threat posed by the Necrons, for they know that should he realise his ambitions, the horrors of a bygone age will once more return to the galaxy.

Imotekh himself understands that the enemies of the Sautekh are many and powerful – perhaps too many to defeat with force of arms alone. As such, the master strategist uses other weapons to bring the galaxy under his control. As he sweeps across the stars, a shadow of terror passes before him – worlds wracked by unnatural storm-laden skies, and scorched by emerald lightning. Armies that march out to meet the Stormlord disappear into his shadow, and so the legend of terror grows. By dark reputation alone have systems surrendered to the Sautekh, preferring a life as slaves of the Necrons to annihilation at the hands of their legions. So it is that the relentless expansion of the Sautekh continues, and Imotekh takes another step towards total domination.

MEPHRIT DYNASTY

Pitiless planet killers, the Mephrit were the solar executioners of the War in Heaven. Stars withered and died under the meticulous attentions of their Crypteks, while their phaerons condemned entire systems to death through hyper-accelerated supernovae. Often, it would be the legions of the Mephrit that the Silent King summoned when a race or planet proved especially defiant, as the dynasty had proved its talent for extermination time and again. Many of the other phaerons considered the Mephrit's methods excessive or distasteful by the ancient codes of warfare. However, the dynasty's victories spoke for themselves, and they swiftly rose in power and prominence.

However, the slow march of the aeons and the Great Sleep has left the Mephrit's grandeur faded and tattered. Their world-rending weapons are lost to the void or fallen into disrepair, while many of their coreworlds are no more. Perhaps most disastrous of all for the Mephrit was the loss of their phaeron, Khyrek the Eternal, who was obliterated along with the dynasty's crownworld by Eldar assassins. In the power vacuum left by their master's demise, many of the Mephrit's Overlords continue to cling to the past, but there are still those who look to future conquests. Among them, Zarathusa the Ineffable gazes upon the ruins of his system and remembers the power he once wielded. Turning his legions once more to the stars, he has set off on a crusade of reclamation. Soon, the galaxy will learn to fear the Mephrit as they did in days of old.

The Mephrit's mastery of exotic energies is boldly displayed in the ranks of their soldiery; the captive light of suns burns within all of the weapons they unleash upon their foes, making the Mephrit instantly recognisable.

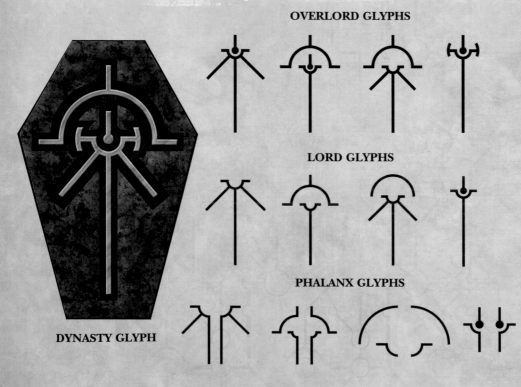

DYNASTY GLYPH

OVERLORD GLYPHS

LORD GLYPHS

PHALANX GLYPHS

The Mephrit have no phaeron to govern them, and their crownworld was lost during the Great Sleep. Now, the Overlords of the dynasty compete for leadership, and many have enhanced their personal glyphs to reflect their self-elevated status.

Originally, the Mephrit's dynastic icon was based upon the constellation formed around their crownworld. However, time and fate has meant that it now bears little resemblance to the Mephrit empire of old.

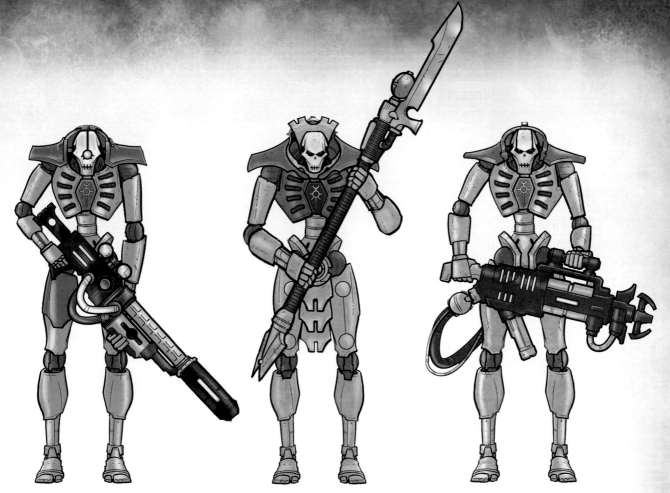

Elite Mephrit soldiery – including even the dynasty's Deathmarks – are permitted to wear the regal green of its rulers.

The heads of Mephrit Lychguard – along with those of many other dynasties – are often entirely white, adding to their skeletal appearance.

The skull-plate honorific of this Mephrit Immortal is a band of stark white, although some phalanxes utilise the dynastic green.

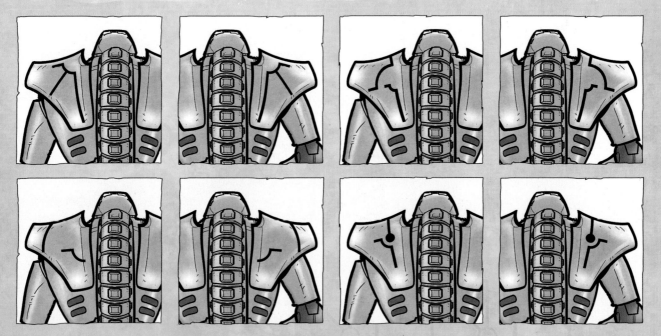

The phalanx glyph employed by a Necron is a simplified version of their Overlord's glyph, which is, in turn, a modification of their dynasty's glyph. Phalanxes are often designated in pairs; each is identified by a glyph which is mirrored on the opposite shoulder of the warriors of their twin phalanx. Above are Necron Warriors of the Mephrit Dynasty from eight phalanxes, displayed in four pairs.

NIHILAKH DYNASTY

Woe to the army that trespasses upon the domains of the Nihilakh. In times of antiquity, the dynasty built vast treasure worlds filled with wealth plundered from a thousand civilisations. Regal in war and glorious in battle, the warriors of Nihilakh have ever worn turquoise and gold as their dynastic colours – both symbolic of wealth and nobility in Necrontyr culture. When the Nihilakh awoke from hibernation it was to find their once-mighty realm in ruins. Looking inward, the dynasty gathered what strength they still possessed to their crownworld, Gheden. Now, they jealously guard the remaining wonders of their empire, and protect the many worlds that make up the constellations of the Nihilakh, shoring up their borders against all intrusion.

It is said that the splendours of the Nihilakh treasure houses eclipse those of all other dynasties combined. Arrogant and proud, the dynasty's Overlords ensure that none forget the great wealth of their people, and so have their Crypteks work precious metals and jewels into the armour of the legions. There are even rumours that some Nihilakh Overlords carry prized relics of the past into battle – borne upon their war engines as reminders of their ancient triumphs.

Greatest among the dynasty's treasures is the Yyth Seer – the preserved head of an alien prophet who was the last of its race. Using neurographic resonators to peer into the prophet's mind, the Overlords have witnessed the future of their race. And it is for this future that the Nihilakh gather their legions for war.

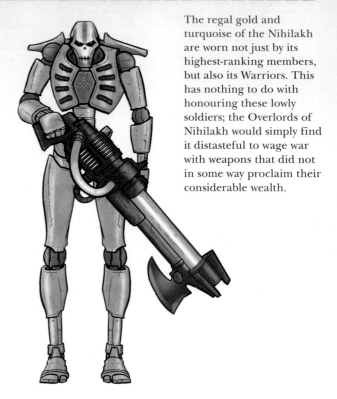

The regal gold and turquoise of the Nihilakh are worn not just by its highest-ranking members, but also its Warriors. This has nothing to do with honouring these lowly soldiers; the Overlords of Nihilakh would simply find it distasteful to wage war with weapons that did not in some way proclaim their considerable wealth.

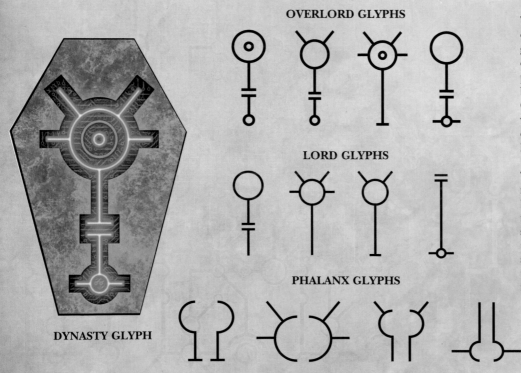

OVERLORD GLYPHS

LORD GLYPHS

PHALANX GLYPHS

DYNASTY GLYPH

The Overlords and Lords of Nihilakh wear personal glyphs reflecting a segment of dynasty's icon – only the phaeron is permitted to bear the icon in its entirety. Often, this personal symbol will signify the part of his dynasty's domain that the lord presides over.

The Nihilakh in particular favour a strict military hierarchy; their phalanx markings are greatly simplified renditions of the dynastic glyph, so as not to detract from the prominence of the nobility's own glyphs.

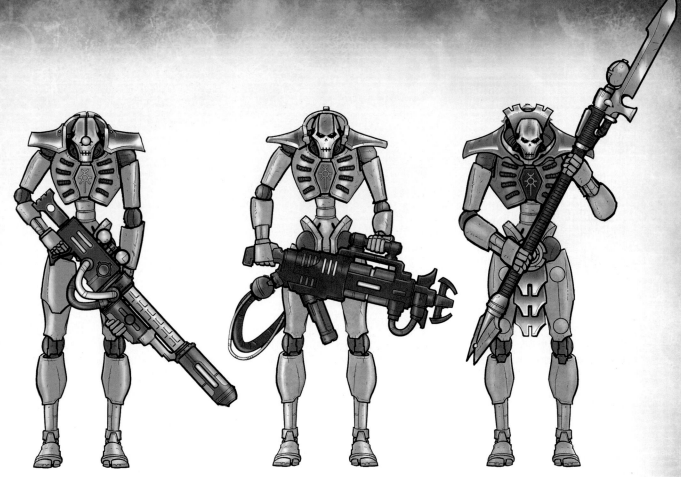

Despite their elite status, Deathmarks operate outside the honourable bounds of warfare. As such, they often omit colours that might otherwise implicate their overseers.

Nihilakh Immortals bear patterns similar to those worn by their dynasty's Warriors, although they are often more intricate or incorporate additional glyphs.

Nihilakh Lychguard traditionally invert the colours and markings which the dynasty's Immortals sport upon their shoulder armour.

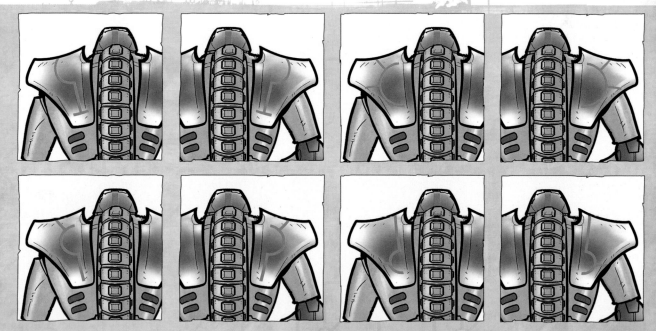

Unlike the more utilitarian designs of some dynasties' phalanx markings, those of the Nihilakh utilise the royal gold and turquoise of their affluent masters. So it is that the pride of the Nihilakh is visible in all strata of their legion organisation.

ANCIENT EMPIRES RETURNED

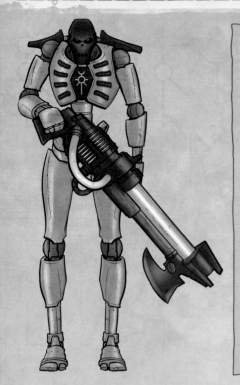

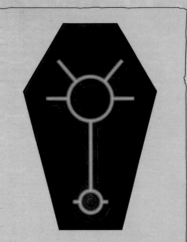

NOVOKH

The crimson armour of the Novokh is a bloody legacy of past victories over the unworthy. Though creatures of living metal long parted with their flesh, the Novokh remember the rites of blooding undertaken by their warriors during the ancient Wars of Secession. The favoured of the Novokh would daub their faces and arms in the blood of those whom they slew in battle, painting spidery patterns of hieroglyphs telling grim tales of carnage and death.

Millennia later, the Novokh still remember these ceremonies, and their Overlords paint their legions crimson in honour of the ritual spilling of blood. To the Warriors and Immortals of the Novokh, this fragment of their past awakens a spark of violent pride and spurs them on to acts of murder.

The symbol of the Novokh reflects the core system cluster of the dynasty, and the six wars of conquest that spread out from its heart. Simpler glyphs of this nature often reflect younger or aggressive expansionist dynasties.

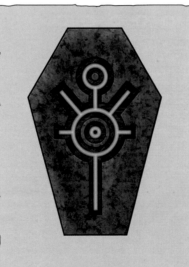

NEPHREKH

The trinary stars of the Nephrekh crownworld glow golden upon the burnished shoulders of its legions. Rich in the solar wealth of scores of systems, the Nephrekh's worlds cluster around the galactic core, its radiant brilliance filling the skies of their tomb worlds with a near-limitless supply of energy. From this golden chalice of flame the warriors of Nephrekh drink deep and grow strong.

Phaeron Sylphek awoke consumed by an obsession with the stars themselves, announcing to his bemused court he wished to drape himself in their molten glory. To placate their lord, the Crypteks of the Nephrekh crafted him a living-gold skin – a gift he has shared with his followers so that they might embody the glory of the triple suns of Nephrekh as they do battle.

At the centre of the Nephrekh dynastic glyph are three overlapping circles representing the three stars of its crownworld.

THOKT

The shifting void rifts of the Hyrakii Deeps hide the coreworlds of the Thokt Dynasty and their legions. Wreathed in sparking blue energy, the crystalline continent-tombs of the Thokt feed upon the power of the rifts, the sky overhead thick with rippling darkness and flickering blue comets. As their armies emerge from their stasis-crypts to bring death to their foes, dull metal skulls reflect the cold sapphire stars far above.

Harnessing this potent radiation, the Thokt Crypteks have fashioned rad-receptors into the weaponry of their soldiers, a symptom of which is the shimmering azure light that emanates from their eyes, gauss flayers and even the cracks in their mechanical forms. When the Thokt gather for war, the barely contained power of the Hyrakii void rifts is ready to be unleashed upon their foes.

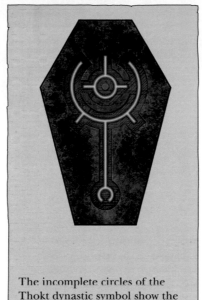

The incomplete circles of the Thokt dynastic symbol show the alignment of the Hyrakii Deeps to the crown and coreworlds of the dynasty's ancestral systems.

CHARNOVOKH

Ravaged by the coming of the Tyranid hive fleets, the legions of Charnovokh cling defiantly to the edges of the Eastern Fringe. Their crypts overrun by the Great Devourer and their tomb worlds defiled by the Imperium, the dynasty musters its extemporary cohorts to gather up the fallen, and awaken the dead for war once more. Lords and Overlords put aside their petty differences, for the fate of their dynasty hangs in the balance.

In honour of their destroyed coreworlds, the Charnovokh bear the colours of Night Unending – dark blue markings upon skull, shoulder and weapon. The higher a Necron's rank within the dynasty, the more blue he wears. As befits his status, Phaeron Thoehk's living metal body is entirely midnight blue, and his form is obscured by a shroud of captive shadow.

Once, the tri-systems and celestial barrier worlds of the Charnovokh were represented in their glyph. Now, only the most central coreworlds of their dynasty remain.

A NEW EPOCH BEGINS

The Necron race is awakening divided in body and purpose. However, from amongst their shattered nobility great leaders are emerging, forging empires from the embers of the old. Every year the Necrons become more numerous, organised and powerful. As bloody madness engulfs the stars, the Necrons may yet sweep the lesser races before them.

744.M41 THE KING RETURNS
The Silent King returns from his self-imposed exile having encountered the Tyranids in the intergalactic void. Realising the threat they pose to the Necrons, he sets about stirring tomb worlds yet to revive. Though he takes pains to conceal his true identity, his influence can be felt throughout the Necron Empire.

781.M41 RISE OF THE STORMLORD
Imotekh takes control of the Sautekh Dynasty. Executing any noble foolish enough to stand in his path, Imotekh cements his position by naming himself phaeron. Within a year of his awakening, the dolmen gates and Tomb Ships of Mandragora are restored, and Imotekh's reconquest of the galaxy begins in earnest.

776.M41 FALLOW WAR

784.M41 THE AWAKENING OF ICNARUS

791.M41 BITTER VINDICATION

The rise of Imotekh the Stormlord has come to pass, proving true the Prophecy of Risen Doom contained within the Book of Mournful Night. With this revelation, the Seer Councils of the craftworlds are forced to concede that the danger prophesied by the Alaitoc Eldar is very real, and set in motion ancient plans to combat them.

888.M41 THE WHISPERING STORM

As the world of Gythos drowns in a full-scale daemonic incursion, the Necrons come to its aid. Null field matrices quieten the raging Warp storms and banish the Daemons. However, the citizens have little time to rejoice before the Necrons begin their deadly harvest.

898.M41 THE SOUL THIEF OF SILENTIA

Legions of the Arotepk march upon the maiden world of Silentia. The Necrons fight their way through an alliance of craftworld Eldar and Harlequins to plunder an ancient gem from the heart of Silentia's world spirit, before vanishing into the void.

799.M41 THE CULL CURTAILED

A huge raiding party of Dark Eldar descends upon the Bardric System to cull its Ork inhabitants, only to find the greenskins gone – slaughtered by awakened legions belonging to the Charnovokh Dynasty. The Necrons provide the Dark Eldar with unexpectedly deadly sport, leaving the survivors to limp back to Commorragh.

873.M41 THE WIDOW'S SPIRAL

The feuding Rytak and Kayra Dynasties each despatch Deathmarks to eradicate the other's court. Such is their success, both worlds are left leaderless.

813.M41 THE SILENT HERALDS

Since the return of the Silent King, the Triarch Praetorians have become aware of his presence in the galaxy once again. Gradually, they have returned to his service, one fragmented host at a time. On this date, the assembled masses of Praetorians officially restore their oaths of fealty to their ancient liege. They will unify the Necron Empire in the face of the Tyranid threat, or face final, lasting death in the attempt.

897.M41 SANCTUARY 101

The armies of the Sautekh Dynasty sweep into Imperial space. Imotekh the Stormlord leads an attack against the fortress convent on Sanctuary 101. The Sisters of Battle within fight valiantly, doing all they can to preserve a record of this previously unknown threat. Yet, for all their defiance, they are slaughtered to the last sister.

855.M41 THE DARKLIGHT EXTINCTION

847.M41 SCOURING OF THE SEERS

Farseers from the craftworld of Alaitoc predict to the day the return of the Hyrekh Dynasty. As soon as the vast stasis-locks protecting the deep Hyrekh war-crypts disengage, and the first Necrons crawl out of the tomb, the Eldar are waiting for them.

899.M41 FEAR HAS A NAME

Following recovery of the pict-capture footage from Sanctuary 101, a number of Inquisitors come to a chilling realisation. Pooling intelligence from dozens of filed, pending or redacted reports – some of which must be reclaimed at gunpoint from the Administratum – they realise the magnitude of this new threat the Imperium.

901.M41 THE REIGN OF IRON STARS

989.M41 PLAGUE OF CLAWS
The Agdagath Dynasty abandons the world of Tyr after it is overrun by Flayed Ones.

973.M41 THE DAMNOS INCIDENT
Legions of the Sautekh Dynasty are awoken by Imperial excavations on the world of Damnos. Even the intervention of the Ultramarines 2nd Company is not enough to save the world from the Necrons.

979.M41 THE BEAST SLAIN
The Tau sept world of Uan'Voss is almost overrun by a sudden infestation of Tyranids, only to be saved by most unlikely rescuers. Several legions of Necrons from the Atun Dynasty fall upon the swarming bio-horrors, Annihilation Barges laying down a crippling bombardment while phalanxes cut their way deep into the horde. Little do the Tau know that they have just witnessed the servants of the Silent King at work.

919.M41 THE DAEMON'S TOMB
The Daemon Prince Shukketh Voidmaw infects the tomb world of Vorketh with the taint of Chaos. Vorketh's regent awakens to find his crypts transformed, and his legions already locked in battle.

926.M41 THE WORLD ENGINE

987.M41 WELL OF TIME
Orikan the Diviner devises a way to better study his enemies. Trapping the Obsidian Glaives 7th Company in a chrono-loop, the Cryptek sends warriors against them and observes the results with curiosity. For the Space Marines, it is a battle that rages on in a day that neither begins nor ends.

912.M41 THE GOD SHADOW
A shard of the Void Dragon escapes from its imprisonment, laying waste to the Arotepk Dynasty in its mindless rage. Though only a faint shadow of a true C'tan, the Void Dragon gorges itself on a dozen worlds, expending its fury upon the living before the Arotepk Crypteks can finally force it back into its cage.

976.M41 THE FEAST OF STEEL
The Sautekh Dynasty expands into Tau space and invades the Kroot-held world of Caroch. Though the Kroot win the first engagements, their attempt to dine upon the living metal of their victims has hideous results as a nano-scarab plague sweeps through their ranks.

947.M41 THE CONQUEST OF UTTU
After his foes refuse his generous terms of surrender, Nemesor Zahndrekh launches a devastating attack upon the planet of Uttu Prime. He is opposed by regiments of Catachans and no less than three companies of Imperial Fists, yet the might of his legions cannot be denied. Uttu becomes another testament to the might of the Necrons.

999.M41 A DYING OF THE LIGHT

Imperial fleets on the edge of Draven Sector become lost in the Warp after an unusual phenomenon causes their Navigators to lose sight of the Astronomican. Investigations uncover the source of the interference upon the tomb world of Petk. Dark Hunters Space Marines launch an assault on the planet, but only minutes after landing all contact with them is lost.

994.M41 THE KILLING GROUND

Waaagh! Bludtoof reaches the fringe worlds of the Thokt Dynasty. The dynasty's lords command the legions to create killing grounds from entire worlds, where the Orks can simply be ground to dust.

990.M41 THE MUSEUM OF DEATH

Trazyn the Infinite creates one of his largest collections to date, sparking the Tyranid invasion of the world of Vuros and then using a temporal cascade to immortalise the event. Even so, Trazyn finds the Tyranids troublesome museum exhibits and is forced to abandon the project after several full-scale battles in the vaults of Solemnace.

993.M41 A DARK EXPERIMENT

By chance, Illuminor Szeras captures a Culexus Assassin during a surprise incursion against a Chaos-held world. Szeras, fascinated by his subject and hungry for further specimens, ensures word reaches the Imperium of the event. The High Lords of Terra do not disappoint, and despatch an Execution Force to destroy the Cryptek.

999.M41 RETURN TO DAMNOS

At great cost, Captain Cato Sicarius, the Ultramarines 2nd Company and their allies, destroy the Necron Lord known as the Undying, and reclaim the world of Damnos for the Imperium.

999.M41 THE FATE OF CRYPTUS

Anrakyr the Traveller and the recently awakened Mephrit of Perdita form a desperate alliance with Dante and the Blood Angels Space Marine Chapter to save their world from Hive Fleet Leviathan.

THE IMMORTAL ARMIES

Under the watchful gaze of the phaerons, the immortal legions of the Necrons march forth to reconquer the stars. Resplendent in their dynastic colours and covered in cryptic hieroglyphs, each army is an echo of a bygone age – a terror returned to wipe the usurper races from the galaxy so that their ancient empire might rise once more to glory.

This Immortal bears the partial symbol of his dynasty upon his shoulder guard to denote his phalanx, the Bloody Tithe.

The Overlord's Lychguard sport an ankh which matches his personal design, in contrast to the common soldiery's.

*Necron Warriors of the Novokh Dynasty are marked in crimson – an echo of their ancient past,
when their flesh-and-blood warriors participated in gory displays of ritual violence.*

Nihilakh Immortals march forth from a Monolith's eternity gate, their ostentatious livery clearly displayed.

From the vantage of his Catacomb Command Barge, the arrogant Nihilakh Overlord Hazeek leads his legions to war.

These Lychguard bear the blank ankh of Nemesor Volkhan, but have been assigned to Hazeek's command to honour an ancient debt.

Impossibly agile, Tomb Blades circle around the rest of the legion like carrion birds, ready to fall upon the foe with their tesla carbines.

Within the silent halls of a tomb world's stasis-crypts, Canoptek Spyders, Scarabs and Wraiths perform tasks of routine maintenance. On the field of battle however, these constructs are equally well-equipped to render down their foes into raw materials for the legions.

The Destroyer cults have but one goal: to cleanse the galaxy of all forms of life. The Triarch Praetorians possess a similar singularity of purpose – though whether the restoration of the Necron Empire is brought about by the death or domination of the lesser races, they care not.

Zarathusa the Ineffable, Overlord of Perdita and
custodian of the Magnovitrium solar mirror

This Triarch Stalker has adopted the distinctive colours of the
Mephrit Dynasty, though its ultimate fealty is to the Silent King.

This Mephrit Immortal advances into battle armed with a fearsome tesla carbine.

Xergyrn, Cryptek of the Mephrit, armed with a staff of light and holding aloft a chronometron

FORCES OF THE NECRONS

The following section contains background and rules information for Necron forces – their deathless warriors, their hyper-advanced vehicles, and the macabre characters that lead them to battle. It enables you to forge your collection of Necron miniatures into an indomitable army ready to conquer all before it in your games of Warhammer 40,000.

CHOOSING AN ARMY

When choosing an army to play a game of Warhammer 40,000, there are two main ways of organising your collection. These are the Unbound method, which means taking whichever units you like, and the Battle-forged method, which is more rigid but has extra benefits. Both are described fully in *Warhammer 40,000: The Rules*.

If you are using the Unbound method, simply use the datasheets later in this section that correspond to the Necron models in your collection. If you are using the Battle-forged method, you will instead need to organise the Necron models in your collection into Detachments. This is a fun process in its own right. The most common of these are the Combined Arms and Allied Detachments. Note that you can also include any of the Formations presented in this section as part of a Battle-forged army.

Furthermore, the Necron Decurion Detachment is a special type of Detachment that can be included in any Battle-forged army. Unlike the Detachments shown in *Warhammer 40,000: The Rules*, it has a Force Organisation Chart whose slots are a combination of specific Formations and Army List Entries instead of Battlefield Roles. However, it still has compulsory and optional elements, as well as Restrictions and Command Benefits, just like any other Detachment.

Although units cannot normally belong to more than one Detachment, units from a Formation that is part of a Necron Decurion Detachment are an exception. They count as part of both their Formation and the Detachment, and have all associated Command Benefits and special rules. If your Warlord is part of a Formation or an Army List Entry that makes up part of a Decurion Detachment, that entire Decurion Detachment is your Primary Detachment.

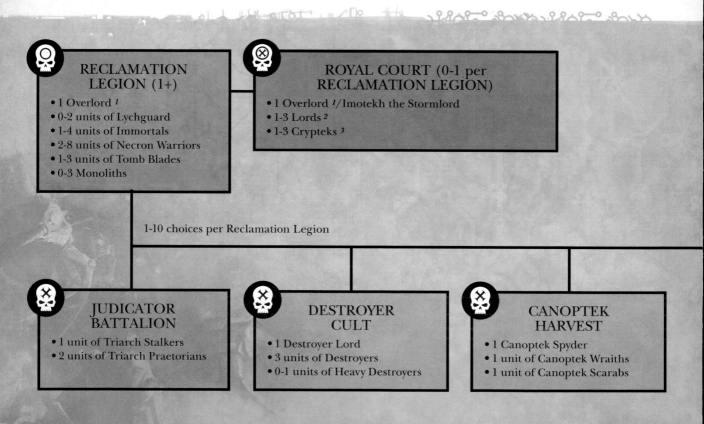

RECLAMATION LEGION (1+)
- 1 Overlord *1*
- 0-2 units of Lychguard
- 1-4 units of Immortals
- 2-8 units of Necron Warriors
- 1-3 units of Tomb Blades
- 0-3 Monoliths

ROYAL COURT (0-1 per RECLAMATION LEGION)
- 1 Overlord *1*/Imotekh the Stormlord
- 1-3 Lords *2*
- 1-3 Crypteks *3*

1-10 choices per Reclamation Legion

JUDICATOR BATTALION
- 1 unit of Triarch Stalkers
- 2 units of Triarch Praetorians

DESTROYER CULT
- 1 Destroyer Lord
- 3 units of Destroyers
- 0-1 units of Heavy Destroyers

CANOPTEK HARVEST
- 1 Canoptek Spyder
- 1 unit of Canoptek Wraiths
- 1 unit of Canoptek Scarabs

1 A Catacomb Command Barge, Nemesor Zahndrekh, Trazyn the Infinite or Anrakyr the Traveller may be taken in place of an Overlord.
2 Vargard Obyron may be taken in place of a Lord.
3 Illuminor Szeras or Orikan the Diviner may be taken in place of a Cryptek.

NECRON DECURION DETACHMENT

The Necron Decurion Detachment allows you to represent the typical structure of the Necron dynasties' armies on the Warhammer 40,000 battlefield. Whether you wish to represent a phaeron leading his crownworld's defence, or a dynasty reclaiming their ancient territories, the choices below will offer a great way to pick your army.

For example, Jon's Necron collection consists of Imotekh the Stormlord, an Overlord, two Lords, a Cryptek, six units of Necron Warriors, six units of Immortals, two units of Tomb Blades, two Doom Scythes, a unit of Deathmarks and a unit of Canoptek Wraiths.

If Jon wishes to organise his collection using the Battle-forged method – as described in Warhammer 40,000: The Rules *– all of his units need to be part of a Detachment or a Formation. Jon achieves this by choosing one Necron Decurion Detachment and one Combined Arms Detachment from* Warhammer 40,000: The Rules.

The Necron Decurion Detachment in Jon's army consists of one Core Formation, one Command Formation and two Auxiliary Formations or Army List Entries. Specifically, it consists of a

Reclamation Legion (his Overlord, all of his Necron Warriors, all of his Tomb Blades and four of his Immortal units), a Royal Court (Imotekh the Stormlord, his Cryptek and one of his Lords), a Deathbringer Flight (both of his Doom Scythes) and a Deathmarks Army List Entry (his Deathmarks unit).

Jon's last two units of Immortals (Troops), his second Lord (HQ) and his Canoptek Wraiths (Fast Attack) form a Combined Arms Detachment. As all of his units belong to a Detachment or a Formation, Jon's army is a Battle-forged army. The units that are part of the Necron Decurion Detachment therefore have the Ever-living Command Benefit, whilst those that are part of the Combined Arms Detachment have the Objective Secured Command Benefit. Finally, Jon chooses Imotekh the Stormlord to be his Warlord – his Necron Decurion Detachment is therefore his Primary Detachment.

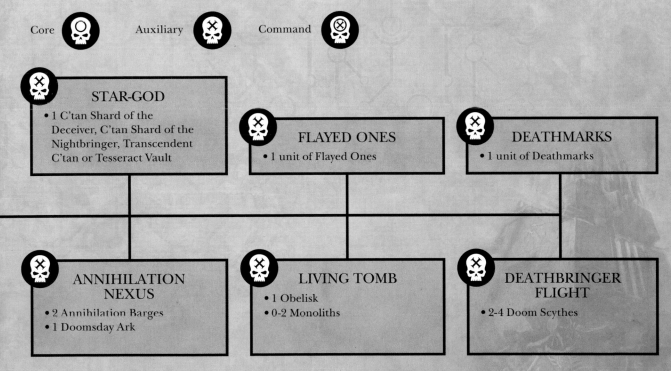

Core   Auxiliary   Command

STAR-GOD
- 1 C'tan Shard of the Deceiver, C'tan Shard of the Nightbringer, Transcendent C'tan or Tesseract Vault

FLAYED ONES
- 1 unit of Flayed Ones

DEATHMARKS
- 1 unit of Deathmarks

ANNIHILATION NEXUS
- 2 Annihilation Barges
- 1 Doomsday Ark

LIVING TOMB
- 1 Obelisk
- 0-2 Monoliths

DEATHBRINGER FLIGHT
- 2-4 Doom Scythes

RESTRICTIONS:
This Detachment must include at least one Core choice. For each Core choice you must include between 1 and 10 Auxiliary choices, in any combination, and you may also include up to one Command choice. Only the datasheets listed above may be included in this detachment.

COMMAND BENEFITS:
Ever-living: Models in this Detachment with the Reanimation Protocols special rule receive a +1 bonus to Reanimation Protocols rolls. Models in this Detachment with the Living Metal rule ignore the effects of Crew Stunned and Crew Shaken (but still lose a Hull Point).

DATASHEETS

Each Necron unit in this book has a datasheet. These detail either Army List Entries or Formations, providing all the rules information that you will need to use your models in your games of Warhammer 40,000.

ARMY LIST ENTRIES

Each Army List Entry contains the following information:

1 **Faction:** *The unit's Faction is shown here by a symbol. All units that have this symbol, which includes all the units described in this book, have the Necrons Faction.*

2 **Battlefield Role:** *The unit's Battlefield Role is shown here by a symbol. Units in this book have one of the following Battlefield Roles: HQ, Troops, Elites, Fast Attack, Heavy Support or Lords of War. The symbols for these Battlefield Roles are defined in Warhammer 40,000: The Rules.*

3 **Unit Name:** *Here you will find the name of the unit.*

4 **Unit Description:** *This section provides a background description of the unit, detailing their particular strengths and weaknesses along with the tactics and methods they employ to wage war in the grim darkness of the 41st Millennium.*

5 **Points Cost:** *This is the points cost of the unit without any upgrades, used if you are choosing an army to a points value.*

6 **Unit Profile:** *This section will show the profiles of any models the unit can include.*

7 **Unit Type:** *This refers to the unit type rules in Warhammer 40,000: The Rules. For example, a unit may be classed as Infantry, Cavalry or Vehicle, which will subject it to a number of rules regarding movement, shooting, assaults, etc.*

8 **Unit Composition:** *This section shows the number and type of models that form the basic unit, before any upgrades are taken.*

9 **Wargear:** *This section details the weapons and equipment the models in the unit are armed with, many of which are described in more detail in the Appendix of this book. The cost for all the unit's basic equipment is included in its points cost.*

10 **Special Rules:** *Any special rules that apply to models in the unit are listed here. Special rules that are unique to models in that unit are described in full here, whilst others are detailed either in the Appendix of this book (pg 112) or in the Special Rules section of Warhammer 40,000: The Rules.*

11 **Options:** *This section lists all of the upgrades you may add to the unit if you wish to do so, alongside the associated points cost for each. Where an option states that you may exchange one weapon 'and/or' another, you may replace either or both, provided you pay the points cost for each. The abbreviation 'pts' stands for 'points' and 'pts/model' stands for 'points per model'. Where applicable, this section also refers to any Transports the unit may take. These have their own datasheets. Dedicated Transports do not use up any slots on a Force Organisation Chart, but otherwise function as separate units. The Detachments section of Warhammer 40,000: The Rules explains how Dedicated Transports work.*

12 **Warlord Traits:** *Sometimes a character's datasheet will have a specific Warlord Trait, in which case it will be listed here.*

13 **Artefacts of the Aeons:** *Some entries have unique items of wargear, the description and rules for which will be listed here.*

FORMATIONS

Formation datasheets are identified by this symbol. The rules for Formations can be found in *Warhammer 40,000: The Rules*. A Formation datasheet will list the Army List Entries which make up the Formation, any restrictions upon what it may include, and any special rules the Formation's units gain.

NECRONS WARGEAR LIST

These lists detail the points values of various items of wargear available to units in your army. Many unit entries in the datasheets that follow may include wargear options from one or more of these lists – in each instance, the datasheet will tell you (in bold text) exactly which of these lists you may use. Rules for these items can be found in the Appendix.

Ranged Weapons.................................pg 113

A model may take one of the following:
- Gauntlet of fire... *10 pts*
- Tachyon arrow.. *25 pts*

Melee Weapons ....pg 115

A model may exchange its staff of light for one of the following:
- Hyperphase sword .... *free*
- Voidblade .... *free*
- Warscythe .... *20 pts*

Technoarcana....................................pg 116

A model may take up to one of each of the following:
- Mindshackle scarabs................................ *10 pts*
- Phylactery .... *15 pts*
- Resurrection orb [2].................................. *25 pts*
- Phase shifter .... *25 pts*

Artefacts of the Aeons........................pg 118

A model may take one of the following:
- The Solar Staff [1] .... *15 pts*
- The Veil of Darkness................................... *25 pts*
- The Gauntlet of the Conflagrator .... *30 pts*
- Voidreaper [1, 2].. *30 pts*
- The Nightmare Shroud .... *35 pts*
- The Orb of Eternity [2]............................ *40 pts*

[1] *Replaces the model's staff of light.*
[2] *May not be taken by Crypteks.*

OVERLORD

80
POINTS

When a Necron Overlord strides forth in his raiment of war, whole worlds quake in terror at his tread. His armoured form is proof against tank-busting weaponry, and his metal sinews have might enough to crush bones to powder. At his command are all the arcane armaments of his ancient civilisation – powerful artefacts that predate many of the galaxy's greatest civilizations. He commands legion upon legion of deathless foot soldiers supported by fleets of arcane war engines, whose only purpose is to obey his every command.

Where biotransference reduced the lower ranks of Necrontyr society to mindless automata, the same process raised the nobility up as cold, calculating demigods of war. Most terrifying of all are the Necron Overlords – beings that hold power in excess even of the Lords that serve them. Such figureheads rule not just worlds, but whole star systems. Their metallic forms are accordingly of an even higher quality, and they possess a strength, resilience, and intellect that few mortals can match.

	WS	BS	S	T	W	I	A	Ld	Sv	Unit Type	Unit Composition
Overlord	5	5	5	5	3	2	3	10	3+	Infantry (Character)	1 Overlord

WARGEAR:
• **Staff of light** (pg 114)

SPECIAL RULES:
• **Independent Character**
• **Reanimation Protocols** (pg 112)

OPTIONS:
• May take items from the **Melee Weapons, Ranged Weapons, Technoarcana** and/or **Artefacts of the Aeons** lists.

LORD

A Tomb World may have dozens or even hundreds of nobles, but only one has the power of absolute rule. For coreworlds and fringeworlds this is usually a Lord, while crownworlds and particularly important coreworlds will have Overlords as their regents. Each phaeron will also lay claim to a crownworld, from which he rules his entire dynasty and from where he will build his armies of reclamation.

These Lords of the Necrons, though lesser in stature and power than an Overlord or phaeron, are nonetheless formidable foes in their own right, and often march to war at the head of a vast mechanical army. Independent of their monarchs, Lords are cunning leaders and pitiless commanders, focused upon the destruction of their foes and their own personal glory. However, when fighting alongside an Overlord or phaeron they will form part of a Royal Court – a terrifying gathering of immortal nobles, each one vying for influence and bent upon completing their own agendas.

	WS	BS	S	T	W	I	A	Ld	Sv	Unit Type	Unit Composition
Lord	4	4	5	5	2	2	2	10	3+	Infantry (Character)	1 Lord

WARGEAR:
• **Staff of light** (pg 114)

SPECIAL RULES:
• **Independent Character**
• **Reanimation Protocols** (pg 112)

OPTIONS:
• May take items from the **Melee Weapons, Ranged Weapons, Technoarcana** and/or **Artefacts of the Aeons** lists.

CRYPTEK

Crypteks bend the forces of the universe to their will, creating impossible technologies and esoteric weaponry to lay waste to armies and destroy worlds. Time, matter and space are their playthings, as they manipulate the atomic structure of their foes or shift the laws of nature to obliterate all who stand before them. The aristocracy of the tomb worlds see them as a necessary evil, granting the Crypteks prestige and status in exchange for their mastery of techno-sorcery, and under the scrutiny of their lord's court they will work their wonders for the Necron armies. However, a Cryptek cares not from whence this favour comes, as long as he has fresh subjects upon which to work his experiments.

	WS	BS	S	T	W	I	A	Ld	Sv	Unit Type	Unit Composition
Cryptek	4	4	4	4	2	2	1	10	4+	Infantry (Character)	1 Cryptek

WARGEAR:
• **Staff of light** (pg 114)

SPECIAL RULES:
• **Independent Character**
• **Reanimation Protocols** (pg 112)

Technomancer: This model and all models with the Reanimation Protocols special rule in his unit receive a +1 bonus to Reanimation Protocols rolls.

OPTIONS:
• May take a chronometron (pg 116) .... *25 pts*
• May take items from the **Technoarcana** and/or **Artefacts of the Aeons** lists.

DESTROYER LORD

110 POINTS

Destroyer Lords are the most maniacal of their kind. This is chiefly because they retain far more intellect than baseline Destroyers, and can bring all of this fearsome intelligence to bear in their pursuit of universal oblivion. Indeed, in a galaxy overspilling with genocidal despots, Destroyer Lords remain worthy of mention as something truly horrific. Where others kill for pleasure, or in service to some malignant god, Destroyer Lords pursue their bloody crusade simply because they can. In this effort they are rarely checked, for they are exceptional combatants and war leaders; their physical strength is monstrous and they possess an excellent – if utterly inscrutable – grasp of strategy.

	WS	BS	S	T	W	I	A	Ld	Sv	Unit Type	Unit Composition
Destroyer Lord	4	4	5	6	3	2	3	10	3+	Jet Pack Infantry (Character)	1 Destroyer Lord

WARGEAR:
- **Staff of light** (pg 114)

SPECIAL RULES:
- **Independent Character**
- **Preferred Enemy**
- **Reanimation Protocols**
  (pg 112)

OPTIONS:
- May take items from the **Melee Weapons, Technoarcana** and/or **Artefacts of the Aeons** lists.

'I ACKNOWLEDGE NO MASTER, SAVE FOR THE ALMIGHTY SPECTRE OF DEATH. IN ITS NAME, I WILL REAP ALL SIGNS OF LIFE FROM THIS GALAXY, LEAVING NOTHING BUT A BARREN MONUMENT TO TIMELESS INEVITABILITY.

CALL IT WHAT YOU WILL, BUT THIS IS THE PURSUIT OF NOTHING LESS THAN ABSOLUTE PERFECTION. THOSE WHO CANNOT UNDERSTAND ITS NECESSITY ARE CLEARLY FLAWED, BUT THEY SHOULD NOT DESPAIR – I WILL ENSURE THAT THEY DO NOT LIVE TO SEE THE FINAL STAGE OF THE WORK COMPLETED.'

- Executioner Ezandrakh of the Mephrit Dynasty, Herald of the Red Harvest

NEMESOR ZAHNDREKH
OVERLORD OF GIDRIM

Nemesor Zahndrekh is counted amongst the greatest Necron generals. Yet, for all his military genius, Zahndrekh does not see reality as it truly is. Having suffered damage during the Great Sleep, his mind is trapped in the distant past, during the Wars of Secession that wracked his corner of the Necrontyr empire. In Zahndrekh's mind, he fights as a creature of flesh and blood, crushing rebellious kings and bringing their domains back into the fold. He does not see armies of Orks, Eldar or humans, but hosts of rebellious kinsmen battling to sunder his beloved dynasty. However, Zahndrekh's battlefield acumen remains undimmed and his armies swift to respond to his commands.

	WS	BS	S	T	W	I	A	Ld	Sv	Unit Type	Unit Composition
Nemesor Zahndrekh	5	5	5	5	3	2	3	10	2+	Infantry (Character)	1 (Unique)

WARGEAR:
- **Staff of light** (pg 114)
- **Phase shifter** (pg 116)

WARLORD TRAIT:
- **Eternal Madness** (pg 112)

SPECIAL RULES:
- **Independent Character**
- **Reanimation Protocols** (pg 112)

Adaptive Tactics: If Nemesor Zahndrekh is your Warlord, you may select a different Warlord Trait for him (no D6 roll is necessary) at the start of each friendly turn after the first – this replaces his existing Warlord Trait. This can be from the table on page 112, or any of the Warlord Traits tables in *Warhammer 40,000: The Rules*. Zahndrekh cannot choose the same Warlord Trait more than once per game.

Counter Tactics: Whilst Nemesor Zahndrekh is within 24" of any enemy unit(s) with any of the following special rules – Counter-attack, Furious Charge, Hit & Run, Split Fire, Stealth, Tank Hunters – then Zahndrekh and his unit also have the same special rule(s).

VARGARD OBYRON
ZAHNDREKH'S SHIELD

Obyron served as Zahndrekh's vargard in their very first campaign – an undignified but hugely successful series of skirmishes in the swamps of Yama – and has stood steadfast at his side ever since, both on the field of battle and off it. Unlike his master, Obyron is very much aware of the changes wrought upon their existence, but has long since abandoned any attempt to awaken Zahndrekh to reality – whatever the fault in his master's mind, the damage lies too deep. So, like any dedicated servant, Obyron attends to all the loose ends created by Zahndrekh's eccentricities, protecting him both from himself and his myriad foes.

	WS	BS	S	T	W	I	A	Ld	Sv	Unit Type	Unit Composition
Vargard Obyron	6	4	5	5	2	2	3	10	2+	Infantry (Character)	1 (Unique)

WARGEAR:
• **Warscythe** (pg 115)

SPECIAL RULES:
• **Independent Character**
• **Reanimation Protocols** (pg 112)

The Vargard's Duty:
Vargard Obyron automatically passes the Initiative test required to make a Glorious Intervention.

Cleaving Counterblow:
When fighting in a challenge, Vargard Obyron gains a bonus Attack for each Attack made by an enemy character against him that fails To Hit. These Attacks are made at the Initiative 1 step (this does not grant an additional Pile In move).

ARTEFACT OF THE AEONS
Ghostwalk Mantle: *An advanced modification of the Veil of Darkness, this artefact can spirit Obyron and any Necrons in close proximity across the battlefield at a command. Nemesor Zahndrekh possesses a homing algorithm synchronised to the mantle, meaning Obyron can lock on to his signal if needed.*

Once per game, at the start of any friendly Movement phase, Vargard Obyron can use the Ghostwalk Mantle to remove himself and his unit from the table if they are not locked in combat. They then immediately arrive anywhere on the board using the rules for Deep Strike. They will not scatter if attempting to Deep Strike within 12" of Nemesor Zahndrekh (this has no effect if Zahndrekh and Obyron are part of the same unit).

ILLUMINOR SZERAS
ARCHITECT OF BIOTRANSFERENCE

The C'tan might have provided the knowledge for biotransference, but it was Szeras who made it a reality. Even then, he saw it as the first of several steps on the path to ultimate evolution that would see him become a god of pure energy. Before this journey can see completion, Szeras must unlock the very secrets of life itself – a goal that yet proves elusive. So it is that his efforts to collect and disassemble every form of life in the galaxy continue apace. A distasteful yet undeniably useful by-product of Szeras' research are his manifold breakthroughs in the field of augmentation. Many Overlords have made use of his skills to improve their underlings' cognitive capacity, bodily resilience or countless other combat systems. In exchange, the Illuminor will claim his pick of living specimens harvested by his latest patron's forces. Szeras frequently takes to the field himself in order to ensure the quality of his living tithe, scuttling into battle with his disturbingly insectile gait and cutting down scores of lesser foes while he coldly selects his next luckless specimens.

	WS	BS	S	T	W	I	A	Ld	Sv	Unit Type	Unit Composition
Illuminor Szeras	4	4	4	4	2	2	4	10	3+	Infantry (Character)	1 (Unique)

WARLORD TRAIT:
- **Immortal Hubris** (pg 112)

SPECIAL RULES:
- **Fear**
- **Independent Character**
- **Reanimation Protocols** (pg 112)

Lord of Technomancy : Illuminor Szeras and all friendly models with the Reanimation Protocols special rule in units within 6" of him, including his own unit, receive a +1 bonus to Reanimation Protocols rolls.

Mechanical Augmentation: At the start of the game, before forces have deployed, nominate one friendly unit of Necron Warriors or Immortals. All models in the nominated unit receive an upgrade for the duration of the game – roll a D6 and consult the following table to determine which upgrade they all have:

1-2   **Hardened Carapace:** The unit is Toughness 5.
3-4   **Improved Optics:** The unit is Ballistic Skill 5.
5-6   **Enhanced Servomotors:** The unit is Strength 5.

ARTEFACT OF THE AEONS

Eldritch Lance: *This stave can emit a blast of furious energy whose passage makes even the air scream in agony.*

Range	S	AP	Type
36"	8	2	Assault 1, Lance

ORIKAN THE DIVINER

SEER OF THE NECRONTYR

Orikan is a consummate astromancer, able to calculate the events of the future from the patterns of the stars. Through careful scrutiny, Orikan can divine great events or small, and advise his allies of the course that fate will take.

Skilled astromancer though he is, Orikan's predictions are not flawless. Unforeseen events and the vagaries of the Warp can wipe out and replace his prophesied timeline. Under such circumstances, Orikan is forced to employ a closely guarded set of chronomantic abilities. Travelling backwards down his own timeline, he emerges in the past at a point at which he can set his version of the future back on track, normally by having the interfering factor destroyed.

Orikan takes great care to keep his machinations hidden from his peers, as suspicion is the last thing he needs at this moment. A thousand millennia of planning is about to come to fruition, and once the stars are in the proper alignment, Orikan will finally embrace his true destiny.

	WS	BS	S	T	W	I	A	Ld	Sv	Unit Type	Unit Composition
Orikan the Diviner	4	4	4	4	2	2	2	10	4+	Infantry (Character)	1 (Unique)
Orikan Empowered	5	5	7	7	4	4	4	10	4+	Infantry (Character)	

WARGEAR:
• **Phase shifter** (pg 116)

SPECIAL RULES:
• **Independent Character**
• **Reanimation Protocols** (pg 112)

Master Chronomancer: Orikan and all models with the Reanimation Protocols special rule in his unit receive a +1 bonus to Reanimation Protocols rolls and can re-roll saving throws of a 1.

The Stars Are Right: Roll a D6 at the start of each friendly turn. If the result is less than the current turn number, Orikan uses the Orikan Empowered profile for the rest of the game. If Orikan suffered an unsaved Wound before becoming empowered, he will have 3 Wounds instead of 4.

WARLORD TRAIT:
• **Enduring Will** (pg 112)

ARTEFACT OF THE AEONS

Staff of Tomorrow: *This staff exists a second ahead of the now, striking Orikan's foes before they even perceive a threat.*

Range	S	AP	Type
-	User	2	Melee, Chronoblade

Chronoblade: The bearer of this weapon re-rolls all failed To Hit rolls in close combat.

ANRAKYR THE TRAVELLER

LORD OF THE PYRRHIAN LEGIONS

Unlike so many of his peers, Anrakyr awoke from his long sleep untainted by madness. Driven by a sense of nobility, Anrakyr gathered his great legions and set out into the stars to unite the dynasties once again. Since that day he has travelled far, obliterating countless alien invaders and awakening one slumbering tomb world after another.

From each world he saves, Anrakyr demands a tithe of warriors to replace the losses he has sustained in his never-ending war of reclamation. The Traveller will requisition these troops by force if he must – a practice that has led to some Overlords branding Anrakyr as a pirate, a bandit and a thief.

Although he awoke with his mind intact, a strange quirk of Anrakyr's revivification has left him able to force his consciousness into the targeting systems of enemy war engines, granting him brief control of the vehicles' weapons. So it is that anyone who takes to the field against Anrakyr should be wary of their own guns, as well as those of their foe.

	WS	BS	S	T	W	I	A	Ld	Sv	Unit Type	Unit Composition
Anrakyr the Traveller	5	5	5	5	3	2	3	10	3+	Infantry (Character)	1 (Unique)

WARGEAR:
- **Tachyon arrow** (pg 114)
- **Warscythe** (pg 115)

WARLORD TRAIT:
- **Implacable Conqueror** (pg 112)

SPECIAL RULES:
- **Counter-attack**
- **Furious Charge**
- **Independent Character**
- **Reanimation Protocols** (pg 112)

Mind in the Machine: At the start of your Shooting phase, choose an enemy vehicle within 12" of Anrakyr the Traveller and roll a D6. On a 4+, randomly select one of that vehicle's weapons (do not include Bombs, weapons with the One Use Only/One Shot Only special rule that have already fired, and weapons that are destroyed). You may then shoot with the selected weapon at another enemy unit. The weapon fires using the vehicle's Ballistic Skill, unless the vehicle is Crew Stunned or Shaken, in which case the weapon can only fire Snap Shots.

Pyrrhian Eternals: At the start of the game, before forces have deployed, nominate one friendly unit of Immortals. All models in the unit have the Furious Charge and Counter-attack special rules.

TRAZYN THE INFINITE
ARCHEOVIST OF THE SOLEMNACE GALLERIES

130
POINTS

When Trazyn the Infinite goes to war, he does so not to destroy, but to preserve. His tomb world of Solemnace is honeycombed with vaults beyond counting, crammed with stasis-frozen curios and remnants of civilisations long dead. Its prismatic galleries are a wonder to behold, containing depictions of many of the galaxy's greatest historical events recreated in hardlight holograms fashioned from hapless living beings.

Though he is rarely as cunning as he might like to believe, Trazyn is nonetheless accomplished at working through nanoscarab-infested thralls. Should he need to act in person, Trazyn the Infinite lives up to his name by pouring his consciousness into one surrogate Necron host after another.

Of late, Trazyn has become ever more frenetic in his efforts at preservation, mobilising all the legions of Solemnace to enact his will. As the flames of war burn ever higher, so more drastic measures are required to save some of the greatest treasures in the galaxy.

	WS	BS	S	T	W	I	A	Ld	Sv	Unit Type	Unit Composition
Trazyn the Infinite	5	5	5	5	3	2	3	10	3+	Infantry (Character)	1 (Unique)

WARLORD TRAIT:
• **Enduring Will** (pg 112)

SPECIAL RULES:
• **Independent Character**
• **Reanimation Protocols** (pg 112)

Surrogate Hosts: If Trazyn is removed as a casualty, roll a D6. On a 2+, choose another friendly Necron Infantry character (excluding Unique models). Remove that model as a casualty and place Trazyn in its place with D3 Wounds remaining. If that character was locked in combat, Trazyn the Infinite is now locked in that combat. If no such characters remain, or a 1 was rolled, remove Trazyn as a casualty as normal.

ARTEFACT OF THE AEONS
Empathic Obliterator: *This stave is rumoured to contain technology designed by the long-vanished Old Ones that has been reverse-engineered with one purpose in mind: the precision extermination of like-minded targets.*

Range	S	AP	Type
-	+2	4	Melee, Concussive, Psionic Shockwaves

Psionic Shockwaves: If a character is slain in a challenge by an attack that has this special rule, all models within 6" of the slain model with the same Faction (friend or foe) immediately suffer a Strength 4 AP- hit.

CATACOMB COMMAND BARGE

Some Necron Overlords fight not on foot, but from the deck of a Catacomb Command Barge – an armoured, repulsor-driven skimmer. The Catacomb Command Barge is a swift and manoeuvrable craft – it has to be, for an Overlord must keep pace with the legions at all times if he is to dictate the flow of battle. More than this, the barge also functions as a giant carrier-wave generator that allows an Overlord to instantaneously issue commands to nearby troops.

Though the Overlord is undeniably the Command Barge's master, he does not operate its controls. Such work is beneath the nobility, and especially below those of such esteemed rank as he. Rather, a pair of Necron Warriors are slaved to the craft's controls, acting as pilots and gunners for the barge's underslung weaponry, leaving their master free to direct his regal attentions to the field at large. Should the Overlord wish to engage his foes in personal combat, the Necron pilots will guide the craft into the ranks of the foe so that their lord might test his blade.

	WS	BS	S	T	W	I	A	Ld	Sv	Unit Type	Unit Composition
Overlord	5	5	5	5	3	2	3	10	3+	Vehicle (Chariot, Skimmer, Fast, Open-topped, Character)	1 Catacomb Command Barge

	⌐Armour¬				
	BS	F	S	R	HP
Catacomb Command Barge	4	11	11	11	3

WARGEAR:
Overlord
- **Staff of light** (pg 114)

Catacomb Command Barge
- **Gauss cannon** (pg 113)
- **Quantum shielding** (pg 115)

SPECIAL RULES:
Overlord
- **Reanimation Protocols** (pg 112)

Catacomb Command Barge
- **Living Metal** (pg 112)

OPTIONS:
- Overlord may take items from the **Melee Weapons, Ranged Weapons, Technoarcana** and/or **Artefacts of the Aeons** lists.
- Catacomb Command Barge may exchange its gauss cannon for a tesla cannon (pg 114)............*free*

Command Wave: All friendly units with the Necrons Faction within 12" of a Catacomb Command Barge re-roll all failed Morale, Pinning and Fear tests. If your Warlord is a Catacomb Command Barge with the Immortal Hubris Warlord Trait, this special rule instead effects all friendly units with the Necrons faction within 18" of your Warlord.

WARRIORS

Remorseless, implacable and armed with terrifying gauss weaponry, legions of Necron Warriors emerge from their stasis-crypts to slay the living. Once, these unfeeling soldiers were the mortal citizens of the Necrontyr, but their flesh was stripped away and forged anew in the ancient past by unfathomable technologies. Necron Warriors are practically unkillable – their living metal bodies are able to heal all but the most grievous of wounds in a matter of moments. Even dismemberment is but a momentary state for a Necron Warrior, as its mangled body reforms itself before the horrified eyes of its enemies. To resist a Necron Warrior is to resist the inevitable onset of death itself.

	WS	BS	S	T	W	I	A	Ld	Sv	Unit Type	Unit Composition
Necron Warrior	4	4	4	4	1	2	1	10	4+	Infantry	10 Necron Warriors

WARGEAR:
• **Gauss flayer** (pg 113)

SPECIAL RULES:
• **Reanimation Protocols** (pg 112)

OPTIONS:
• May include up to ten additional Necron Warriors.. *13 pts/model*
• May select a Ghost Ark (pg 87) or Night Scythe (pg 86) as a Dedicated Transport.

IMMORTALS

Even before biotransference, the Immortals were the elite soldiers of the Necrontyr and marched at the forefront of their galactic conquests. Reborn into tireless metal bodies, they are now the shock troops of each tomb world's armies. Where Necron Warriors are but fodder to be fed to the guns of the foe, Immortals are far more valuable to their Overlords and will be deployed accordingly. Heavily armed and armoured, they will stop at nothing in the completion of their masters' goals, and will often be found at the heart of any crushing offensive or punitive counter-attack. The Immortal legions are but an echo of what they once were, for trillions were destroyed in the final days of the War in Heaven. However, billions more survived, and now wait only to be awakened from their tombs to begin the reconquest of the galaxy.

	WS	BS	S	T	W	I	A	Ld	Sv	Unit Type	Unit Composition
Immortal	4	4	4	4	1	2	1	10	3+	Infantry	5 Immortals

WARGEAR:
• Gauss blaster (pg 113)

SPECIAL RULES:
• **Reanimation Protocols** (pg 112)

OPTIONS:
• May include up to five additional Necron Immortals .... *17 pts/model*
• The entire squad may exchange their gauss blasters for tesla carbines (pg 114) .... *free*
• May select a Night Scythe (pg 86) as a Dedicated Transport.

LYCHGUARD

Tireless, deadly and loyal, Lychguard are ideal bodyguards and lieutenants for their Overlord masters. Physically, Lychguard are incredibly imposing, housed in the heavily armoured forms commonly reserved for Necron royalty. Their very appearance is a brazen challenge to the foe – one that the Lychguard are more than capable of making good on – and they will often form the lynchpin that anchors a Necron battle line in place. As with much of the Necron army, a Lychguard's armament is decreed largely by tradition. Most are equipped with heavy-bladed warscythes, though phalanxes employed by more influential Overlords may instead carry hyperphase swords and dispersion shields. Regardless of armament, Lychguard are self-aware enough to take pride in their bloody work.

	WS	BS	S	T	W	I	A	Ld	Sv	Unit Type	Unit Composition
Lychguard	4	4	5	5	1	2	2	10	3+	Infantry	5 Lychguard

WARGEAR:
• **Warscythe** (pg 115)

SPECIAL RULES:
• **Reanimation Protocols** (pg 112)

OPTIONS:
• May include up to five additional Lychguard.. *25 pts/model*
• The entire unit may exchange their warscythes for hyperphase swords (pg 115) and dispersion shields (pg 116) .... *5 pts/model*
• May select a Night Scythe (pg 86) as a Dedicated Transport.

DEATHMARKS

For millennia, Deathmarks have served the Necron nobility as snipers and assassins. These deadly marksmen seldom take position with the rest of the army. Instead, they slip sideways out of reality and monitor the conflict from a hyperspace oubliette – a pocket dimension riding the gap between the then and now. The Deathmarks track enemy communication channels, teleport beams and orbital descents in order to select suitably high-profile prey. This done, they exit their oubliette to tag their quarry with the hunter's mark from which they take their name – an eerie green energy halo that plays about the target's head in five dimensions. Though this mark will last an hour at most, the Deathmarks will never lose track of their prey while it endures, though few survive even seconds once locked in the Deathmarks' sights.

	WS	BS	S	T	W	I	A	Ld	Sv	Unit Type	Unit Composition
Deathmark	4	4	4	4	1	2	1	10	3+	Infantry	5 Deathmarks

WARGEAR:
• **Synaptic disintegrator** (pg 114)

SPECIAL RULES:
• **Deep Strike**
• **Reanimation Protocols** (pg 112)

Hunters from Hyperspace: During the player turn in which this unit arrives from Deep Strike Reserve, all shooting attacks made by the Deathmarks in this unit will wound on To Wound rolls of 2+, regardless of the victim's Toughness.

Ethereal Interception: If this unit is in Deep Strike Reserve, immediately after an enemy unit arrives from Deep Strike Reserve this unit may choose to immediately arrive using the rules for Deep Strike (if this unit does not enter play in this manner, make Reserve Rolls for it as normal in subsequent turns). At the end of that enemy Movement phase, any friendly Deathmarks unit that arrived on the board in this manner during that turn may fire its weapons at any enemy unit that arrived from Reserves that phase; any Deathmarks unit that does so cannot fire its weapons in its following turn.

OPTIONS:
• May include up to five additional Deathmarks................. *18 pts/model*
• May select a Night Scythe (pg 86) as a Dedicated Transport.

FLAYED ONES

Flayed Ones are flesh-eating carrion creatures, the victims of a terrible madness that took root during the last days of the War in Heaven. Other Necrons loathe the Flayed Ones, and will banish them to a foul charnel pocket-dimension for fear of the disease they carry. Yet though the Necrons will not suffer Flayed Ones to march at their side, little can be done to prevent them crawling through the dimensional meniscus to fall upon a battle already underway. Flayed Ones can materialise at any time, lured from their bleak dimension by the scent of blood and carnage, and will commonly stalk their prey before attacking with little regard for strategy. When the moment to strike comes, Flayed Ones scramble madly into battle, slashing at their prey with twisted talons and draping themselves in the mangled body parts of their quarry.

	WS	BS	S	T	W	I	A	Ld	Sv	Unit Type	Unit Composition
Flayed One	4	1	4	4	1	2	3	10	4+	Infantry	5 Flayed Ones

WARGEAR:
• **Two flayer claws** (pg 115)

SPECIAL RULES:
• **Deep Strike**
• **Fear**
• **Infiltrate**
• **Reanimation Protocols**
  (pg 112)

OPTIONS:
• May include up to fifteen additional Flayed Ones .... *13 pts/model*

'THROUGH TECHNOLOGY WE THOUGHT TO DEFEAT THE NATURAL ORDER. BUT THE ONSET OF ETERNITY CANNOT BE DENIED FOREVER; THE UNIVERSE WILL SEE US HUMBLED FOR OUR PRESUMPTION. YET ITS METHODS OF ATTACK ARE LIMITED. WE LONG AGO REMOVED OUR BODIES FROM MORTALITY'S GRASP AND BARTERED AWAY OUR SOULS FOR TECHNOLOGICAL BAUBLES AND THE TRAPPINGS OF POWER. OUR MINDS, THEN, ARE ALL THAT REMAINS FOR US TO LOSE, AND IT IS HERE THAT THE NEXT STROKE AGAINST US WILL FALL. THOUGH OUR INDIVIDUAL AFFLICTIONS MAY TAKE DIFFERENT FORMS, SOONER OR LATER WE WILL BE LOST TO MADNESS.'

- Szarekh, Last of the Silent Kings

TRIARCH PRAETORIANS

The Triarch Praetorians are the ancient law keepers of the Necron race, peerless warriors charged with the survival of the dynasties and the primacy of the ancient Necrontyr codes. None fought harder or with more devotion during the War in Heaven, yet it seemed that the Praetorians had failed in their ancient duty. Now, however, as their race awakes from its millennial slumber, the Praetorians move between the tomb worlds with fresh purpose, for in Necron victory lies the Praetorians' redemption. Even could he do so, no noble would refuse such assistance, for extreme age has done little to dull the Triarch Praetorians' combat skills. Launching into battle on gravity displacement packs, the Triarch Praetorians will plunge into the thick of the fighting to wreak utter havoc upon their foes.

	WS	BS	S	T	W	I	A	Ld	Sv	Unit Type	Unit Composition
Triarch Praetorian	4	4	5	5	1	2	2	10	3+	Jump Infantry	5 Triarch Praetorians

WARGEAR:
• **Rod of covenant** (pg 113)

SPECIAL RULES:
• **Fearless**
• **Reanimation Protocols**
  (pg 112)

OPTIONS:
• May include up to five additional Triarch Praetorians .... *28 pts/model*
• The entire unit may exchange their rods of covenant for voidblades (pg 115)
  and particle casters (pg 113) ....*free*
• May select a Night Scythe (pg 86) as a Dedicated Transport.

TRIARCH STALKERS

125 POINTS

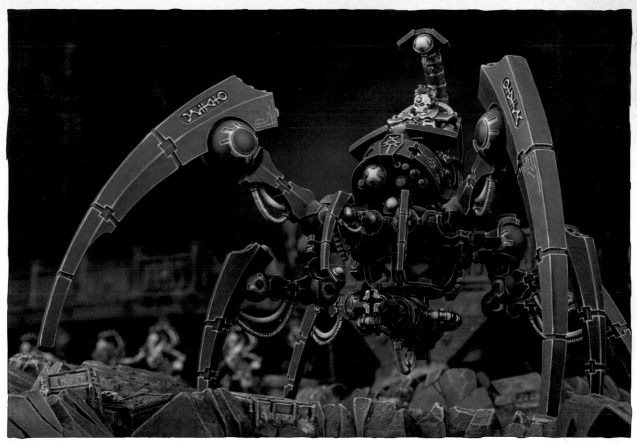

Like an enormous spider, a Triarch Stalker looms over the battlefield, its devastating weaponry directed by a high-ranking Triarch Praetorian. When a Triarch Stalker advances, it does so with a speed and surety that belies its jerking gait. Indeed, it can cover all manner of terrain with a deftness and precision seldom found in the walkers of less advanced races. Capable of operating as an opportunist tank hunter or flushing infantry from dense – and otherwise impassable – terrain, the Triarch Stalker is a versatile and mobile weapons platform. Its pilot will direct his every effort to augmenting the efforts of nearby Necron forces, overriding their targeting protocols with augmentative data on priority victims. In this way, the Triarch Stalkers bolster the Necron line wherever it meets the greatest resistance.

	WS	BS	S	F	S	R	I	A	HP	Unit Type	Unit Composition
Triarch Stalker	4	4	7	11	11	11	2	3	3	Vehicle (Walker, Open-topped)	1 Triarch Stalker

WARGEAR:
- **Heat ray** (pg 114)
- **Quantum shielding** (pg 115)

SPECIAL RULES:
- **Living Metal** (pg 112)
- **Move Through Cover**

Targeting Relay: All friendly non-vehicle units with the Necrons Faction within 6" of at least one Triarch Stalker add 1 to their Ballistic Skill, unless they are firing Snap Shots.

OPTIONS:
- May include up two additional Triarch Stalkers.. *125 pts/model*
- Any model may exchange its heat ray for one of the following:
  - Particle shredder (pg 113) .... *5 pts*
  - Twin-linked heavy gauss cannon (pg 113) .... *10 pts*

83

C'TAN SHARD OF THE NIGHTBRINGER

The doom of stars and the demise of worlds, the Shard of the Nightbringer is death incarnate. When unleashed upon the battlefield, it manifests as a towering cloaked reaper that shines with a dark light – an image that resonates deeply in the primal subconscious of many of the lesser races. All who look upon the shard feel the cold fingers of death upon their throats, for in its terrible and majestic form is the inevitability of their destruction.

Legends tell of the Nightbringer as the first and most powerful of the C'tan. In ancient hiero-scripts it is depicted as an ever-hungering god of death, feasting upon the pain and anguish of entire species. Star systems, planets and civilisations have all fallen before its dark scythe, and even the Necrons fear its coming. Millions of years after the demise of the C'tan, shards of the Nightbringer remain the most dangerous and difficult to control for the Necrons. Somewhere deep within these fragments linger the memories of the Nightbringer as it was, and its unending hatred of the race that betrayed it.

	WS	BS	S	T	W	I	A	Ld	Sv	Unit Type	Unit Composition
C'tan Shard of the Nightbringer	6	4	7	7	4	4	4	10	4+	Monstrous Creature (Character)	1 (Unique)

WARGEAR:
• Powers of the C'tan (pg 117)

SPECIAL RULES:
• Eternal Warrior
• Fearless
• Fleshbane

Immune to Natural Law: When moving, this model can move over all other models and terrain as if they were open ground, and automatically passes Dangerous Terrain tests. However, it cannot end its move on top of other models and can only end its move on top of impassable terrain if it is possible to actually place the model on top of it.

Necrodermis: This model has a 4+ invulnerable save. If it is ever reduced to 0 Wounds, before removing the model as a casualty, each nearby unit (friend or foe) suffers a Strength 4 AP1 hit for each model it has within D6" of this model.

Gaze of Death: In its Shooting phase, in addition to using Powers of the C'tan, this model can target one non-vehicle enemy unit within 12" to which it has line of sight. The unit suffers a number of Wounds equal to 3D6 minus its Leadership, resolved at AP2 and with the Ignores Cover special rule. If at least one unsaved Wound is inflicted, the C'tan Shard of the Nightbringer immediately regains one Wound lost earlier in the battle.

C'TAN SHARD OF THE DECEIVER

240 POINTS

A master of mistrust and lies, the Shard of the Deceiver entangles his foes in webs of illusion in order to lead them to their doom. Reality and perception are its playthings – the god-fragment prefers misdirection and trickery to outright force, taking pleasure in turning its foes against one another, or wallowing in their despair before finally crushing the life from their frail bodies. Falsehoods uttered by the shard have plunged whole systems into crippling civil war, and even seen entire species become prematurely extinct.

If the Nightbringer was reputed to be the oldest and most powerful of the C'tan, then the Deceiver was without doubt the most cunning. Stories from the Time of Flesh and the coming of the C'tan tell of the Deceiver's audience with the Silent King. In the Necrontyr's darkest hour, when they faced annihilation at the hands of the Old Ones, it was the Deceiver that offered up the secrets of biotransference. A curse disguised as a tempting gift, this would prove to be the Necrontyr's doom, and the C'tan would feast upon their remains.

	WS	BS	S	T	W	I	A	Ld	Sv	Unit Type	Unit Composition
C'tan Shard of the Deceiver	5	5	7	7	4	4	4	10	4+	Monstrous Creature (Character)	1 (Unique)

WARGEAR:
• Powers of the C'tan (pg 117)

SPECIAL RULES:
• Eternal Warrior
• Fearless
• Hit & Run

Immune to Natural Law: When moving, this model can move over all other models and terrain as if they were open ground, and automatically passes Dangerous Terrain tests. However, it cannot end its move on top of other models and can only end its move on top of impassable terrain if it is possible to actually place the model on top of it.

Necrodermis: This model has a 4+ invulnerable save. If it is ever reduced to 0 Wounds, before removing the model as a casualty, each nearby unit (friend or foe) suffers a Strength 4 AP1 hit for each model it has within D6" of this model.

Dread: Models in enemy units that are within 12" this model subtract 2 from their Leadership characteristic.

Grand Illusion: Immediately after all forces have deployed and all Scout redeployments have been made, you may remove this model and/or up to D3 other friendly units within 12" of it from the table. Each unit that is removed in this manner can either be immediately deployed again using the normal Deployment rules, or placed in Reserve.

NIGHT SCYTHE

The Night Scythe is the Necrons' favoured tool of invasion, a sickle-winged herald of woe that possesses the ability to beam Necrons directly into battle. Manoeuvrable enough to evade orbital defences and interceptors, and swift enough to outpace mustering foes, Night Scythes can ghost through a defence perimeter to deploy invasion forces well behind enemy lines. Unlike the armoured carriers employed by other races, the Night Scythe does not have a transport compartment as such. Instead, it deploys troops by means of a captive wormhole, whose point of origin is anchored on a distant tomb world. Utilising technologies beyond the comprehension of the galaxy's lesser races, these invasion beams allow the Night Scythe to fulfil the role of a conventional transport vehicle, yet without ever placing its 'passengers' at risk.

	BS	F	S	R	HP	Unit Type	Unit Composition
Night Scythe	4	11	11	11	3	Vehicle (Flyer, Transport)	1 Night Scythe

(Armour columns: F, S, R)

WARGEAR:
• **Twin-linked tesla destructor** (pg 114)

SPECIAL RULES:
• **Living Metal** (pg 112)
• **Supersonic**

Invasion Beams: A unit that begins its Movement phase embarked upon a Night Scythe can disembark either before or after it has moved (including pivoting on the spot), even though it is Zooming, so long it has not moved more than 36" in that Movement phase. If a unit disembarks from a Night Scythe after it has moved 24" or more, models in the unit can only fire Snap Shots until the start of their next turn. Units embarked on a Night Scythe ignore all effects of damage on passengers. If a Night Scythe is destroyed, the units embarked upon it suffer no damage or ill effects – instead they are immediately placed into Ongoing Reserves.

TRANSPORT:
• **Transport Capacity:** Fifteen models.
• **Fire Points:** None.
• **Access Points:** A Night Scythe has one Access Point on the underside of its hull.

GHOST ARK

Ghost Arks are tasked with trawling for remnants of Necrons unable to self-repair. Recovered components are set upon by swarms of constructor scarabs that return the fallen Necrons to full function. Repaired warriors are then locked in stasis until the Ghost Ark is at capacity, at which point it will either return its cargo to their tomb world or else deploy them directly into battle. Ghost Arks are often used as conventional transports that ferry reinforcements into battle – however, they truly come into their own once their grim cargo has disembarked. Drifting behind the ranks of Necrons, the Arks flicker with emerald energies as they repair one fallen foot soldier after another. The enemy can only watch with dawning horror as their best efforts to slay the Necrons are undone.

	Armour					Unit Type	Unit Composition
	BS	F	S	R	HP		
Ghost Ark	4	11	11	11	4	Vehicle (Skimmer, Open-topped, Transport)	1 Ghost Ark

WARGEAR:
- **Two gauss flayer arrays** (pg 113)
- **Quantum shielding** (pg 115)

SPECIAL RULES:
- **Living Metal** (pg 112)

Repair Barge: At the start of each friendly Movement phase, this model can repair fallen Necron Warriors. To do so, nominate a friendly unit of Necron Warriors that is either within 6" of this model or embarked upon it, and roll a D3. Add a number of Necron Warriors to the unit equal to the result – this cannot take the unit beyond its starting size nor, if it is currently embarked in the Ghost Ark, beyond the vehicle's Transport Capacity (any excess are destroyed). These Necron Warriors must be placed within 6" of the Ghost Ark, or if the unit is currently embarked in the Ghost Ark, within it. If a model cannot be placed for any reason, it is destroyed. Necron Warriors repaired in this manner can move and act normally this turn.

TRANSPORT:
- **Transport Capacity:** Ten models. It can only carry Necron Warriors and Necron characters with the Infantry unit type.

CANOPTEK WRAITHS

Canoptek Wraiths flit across the battlefield like the spectres of the restless dead. Using their dimensional destabilisation matrices, these strange constructs are able to phase in and out of reality at will. This unique technology means that, though no more than mindless drones, Canoptek Wraiths have manifold uses in war. Fortifications are no obstacle to a Wraith, and they are able to pass more or less undetected even through the midst of the foe, making them exceptional spies and assassins both. Furthermore, Canoptek Wraiths make effective terror-troops, appearing as if from nowhere to strike at vital targets in the enemy's midst. Here, swirling through the panicked gunfire of the foe, the Wraiths flicker rapidly in and out of phase with reality, shots and blades passing harmlessly through their indistinct forms.

	WS	BS	S	T	W	I	A	Ld	Sv	Unit Type	Unit Composition
Canoptek Wraith	4	4	6	5	2	2	3	10	3+	Beasts	3 Canoptek Wraiths

SPECIAL RULES:
- **Fearless**
- **Rending**
- **Very Bulky**

Wraith Form: Canoptek Wraiths have a 3+ invulnerable save.

Wraithflight: When moving, Canoptek Wraiths can move over all other models and terrain as if they were open ground. However, they cannot end their move on top of other models and can only end their move on top of impassable terrain if it is possible to actually place the models on top of it.

OPTIONS:
- May include up to three additional Canoptek Wraiths .... *40 pts/model*
- Any model may take one of the following:
  - Whip coils (pg 115) .... *3 pts/model*
  - Particle caster (pg 113) .... *5 pts/model*
  - Transdimensional beamer (pg 114) .... *10 pts/model*

CANOPTEK SCARABS

Canoptek Scarabs sweep across the battlefield in vast, undulating swarms that devour all in their path. Mindless feeding machines, the Scarabs are constructs designed to break down matter into raw energy that can then be woven into fresh forms. Within the confines of a tomb this process is one of clearing and manufacture, but on the battlefield it is a powerful force of destruction. Many Overlords will send their Scarabs sweeping ahead of their army, forcing foes to waste ammunition fending them off. Lesser soldiers may be driven mad, or even overwhelmed and devoured by endless waves of the worker-constructs. However, it is against the enemy's armour that Canoptek Scarabs truly come into their own – once they have latched onto a vehicle, they will break down even the thickest hull plating with alarming speed.

	WS	BS	S	T	W	I	A	Ld	Sv	Unit Type	Unit Composition
Canoptek Scarabs	2	2	3	3	3	2	4	10	6+	Beasts	3 Canoptek Scarab bases

SPECIAL RULES:
• **Fearless**
• **Swarms**

Entropic Strike: If a model has this special rule, or is attacking with a Melee weapon that has this special rule, a To Wound roll of a 6 Wounds automatically, regardless of the target's Toughness. Against vehicles and buildings, an Armour Penetration roll of 6 that does not cause a penetrating hit automatically causes a glancing hit.

OPTIONS:
• May include up to six additional Canoptek Scarab bases............................ *20 pts/base*

TOMB BLADES

Tomb Blades are fast moving, single-pilot attack craft that hurtle across the battlefield in seemingly erratic swarms. Originally designed as spacefighters during the final days of the War in Heaven, these peculiar skimmers have since been pressed into service as far-ranging ground attack units. Squadrons of Tomb Blades strike at lightly defended positions, supply convoys and other targets of opportunity, or else swarm around the flanks of the main Necron army to encircle the foe. Thanks to their dimensional repulsor engines and the mechanical hardiness of their crew, Tomb Blades are able to corkscrew madly across the battlefield in a way no living pilot could replicate – or even survive. Their attack vectors disrupt the enemy's aim, leaving the Necron pilot free to target the foe with blistering salvoes of gauss fire.

	WS	BS	S	T	W	I	A	Ld	Sv	Unit Type	Unit Composition
Tomb Blade	4	4	4	5	1	2	1	10	4+	Jetbike	3 Tomb Blades

WARGEAR:
• **Twin-linked gauss blaster**
  (pg 113)

SPECIAL RULES:
• **Reanimation Protocols** (pg 112)

OPTIONS:
• May include up to seven additional Tomb Blades..*18 pts/model*
• Any model may exchange its twin-linked gauss blasters for:
  - Twin-linked tesla carbines (pg 114) ....*free*
  - Particle beamer (pg 113) ....*2 pts/model*
• Any model may take shieldvanes (pg 116) .... *2 pts/model*
• Any model may take one of the following:
  - Shadowloom (pg 116) ....*1 pt/model*
  - Nebuloscope (pg 116) ....*2 pts/model*

The Destroyers' chilling dedication to destruction is a valuable addition to any Necron army. They are deranged agents of annihilation whose sole reason for existence is centred around an unshakeable yearning to quench the flames of life. For a Destroyer, everything is subsumed into the all-important goal of extermination. They ruthlessly adapt, augment or expunge any facet of their physical form if it will improve their mission of slaughter. Legs are removed in favour of repulsor platforms, arms are fused to the workings of gauss cannons. Even the Destroyer's senses are reconfigured to better serve target lock and prediction capability, its neural circuitry repathed to improve response times at the cost of vestigial emotions. A Destroyer draws no distinctions between combatants and civilians – all life is its enemy.

	WS	BS	S	T	W	I	A	Ld	Sv	Unit Type	Unit Composition
Destroyer	4	4	4	5	2	2	1	10	3+	Jet Pack Infantry	1 Destroyer
Heavy Destroyer	4	4	4	5	2	2	1	10	3+	Jet Pack Infantry	

WARGEAR:
- **Gauss cannon**
  (Destroyer only) (pg 113)
- **Heavy gauss cannon**
  (Heavy Destroyer only) (pg 113)

OPTIONS:
- May include up to five additional Necron Destroyers .... *40 pts/model*
- May upgrade one Destroyer to a Heavy Destroyer... *10 pts*

SPECIAL RULES:
- **Preferred Enemy**
- **Reanimation Protocols** (pg 112)
- **Very Bulky**

HEAVY DESTROYERS

50 POINTS

Armed with oversized gauss cannons, Heavy Destroyers send blazing energy blasts searing across the battlefield. These heavily armed adherents of the Destroyer Cults glide across scorched earth scanning for victims, the flickering light of their weapons' energy cores echoing the cold hatred in their optics. When a Heavy Destroyer's targeting lens focuses upon an enemy, the battlefield recedes in its mind until only hunter and prey remain, the compulsion to kill drowning out everything else. Few things escape intact from the cold, unrelenting fury of a Heavy Destroyer once it has designated its target – even after its heavy gauss cannon has disabled a tank, the Destroyer will continue to hammer it with fire, tearing apart the twisted hull and incinerating crewmen even as they try to scramble free of the burning wreck.

	WS	BS	S	T	W	I	A	Ld	Sv	Unit Type	Unit Composition
Heavy Destroyer	4	4	4	5	2	2	1	10	3+	Jet Pack Infantry	1 Heavy Destroyer

WARGEAR:
• Heavy gauss cannon

SPECIAL RULES:
• Preferred Enemy
• Reanimation Protocols (pg 112)
• Very Bulky

OPTIONS:
• May include up to two additional Heavy Destroyers.....................................50 pts/model

92

CANOPTEK SPYDERS

50 POINTS

Though essentially an automated drone, a Canoptek Spyder is nonetheless a formidable foe. Its vast array of self-repair and backup systems – vital for enduring uncaring millennia – offer substantial protection against incoming fire. In return, any enemy that strays within reach of the Canoptek Spyder will have flesh scoured from bone by a multitude of mechanical tools and pincers. Furthermore, every Canoptek Spyder can craft slaved hosts of Canoptek Scarabs within its abdomen, sending them swarming out to devour the foe. Some – those charged with guarding their slumbering Necron masters – mount particle beamers in place of claws, allowing them to blast their victims clean out of existence. Others, meanwhile, are equipped with thrumming gloom prisms that render enemy psykers all but helpless in battle.

	WS	BS	S	T	W	I	A	Ld	Sv	Unit Type	Unit Composition
Canoptek Spyder	3	3	6	6	3	2	2	10	3+	Monstrous Creature	1 Canoptek Spyder

SPECIAL RULES:
• **Fearless**

Scarab Hive: Once per friendly Movement phase, each Canoptek Spyder can use this special rule to create Canoptek Scarabs. To do so, nominate a friendly unit of Canoptek Scarabs that is within 6" of the Canoptek Spyder. Add a single Canoptek Scarab base to the unit – this can take the unit beyond its starting size, but must be placed within 6" of the Canoptek Spyder. If a model cannot be placed for any reason, it is destroyed. Canoptek Scarabs created in this manner can move and act normally this turn. Roll a D6 each time a Canoptek Spyder uses its Scarab Hive special rule, immediately after placing any Canoptek Scarabs that were created – on a roll of a 1 the Canoptek Spyder suffers a single Wound with no saves of any kind allowed.

OPTIONS:
• May include up to two
  additional Canoptek Spyders................................. *50 pts/model*
• Any model may take a fabricator
  claw array (pg 116) .... *5 pts/model*
• Any model may take a gloom prism (pg 116) ...... *10 pts/model*
• Any model may take a
  twin-linked particle beamer (pg 113) .... *10 pts/model*

DOOM SCYTHE

160
POINTS

Doom Scythes are heralds of terror and dismay. These supersonic fighter craft range ahead of a Necron army, drawing upon their strategic datastacks to operate with virtual autonomy. Whether performing terror-raids as a precursor to invasion, keeping the air free of enemy aircraft, or launching overwhelming strike missions against key strategic targets, Doom Scythe pilots will complete their task with merciless precision. The unearthly howl of the Doom Scythes can scatter its foes, such is the terror it sows. Though shrewd Overlords will use this effect to their advantage, the greatest weapon in the Doom Scythe's arsenal is its infamous death ray. Capable of ploughing a searing furrow through infantry, tanks and even towering bastions, these horrific weapons have given the Doom Scythe a dire reputation indeed.

	⌐Armour⌐					Unit Type	Unit Composition
	BS	F	S	R	HP		
Doom Scythe	4	11	11	11	3	Vehicle (Flyer)	1 Doom Scythe

WARGEAR:
- **Death ray** (pg 113)
- **Twin-linked tesla destructor** (pg 114)

SPECIAL RULES:
- **Living Metal** (pg 112)
- **Supersonic**

MONOLITH

A veritable floating fortress, the Monolith embodies the implacable might of the Necrons. Hovering aloft on rumbling repulsor units, each Monolith can unleash an immense amount of firepower, and is so resilient as to seem nigh invulnerable to conventional weaponry. Furthermore, its target matrices, motive units, power conduits and command nodes are all capable of comprehensive self-repair. So durable and deadly is the Monolith that it is most Overlords' first choice to spearhead a full-scale planetary invasion. Drifting down from the heavens whilst spitting arcing blasts of particle energy, the Monolith brings death and destruction on a massive scale. Yet it is only when each Monolith's eternity gate yawns wide and begins to disgorge rank upon rank of Necron soldiery that the enemy truly know despair.

		┌Armour┐					
	BS	F	S	R	HP	Unit Type	Unit Composition
Monolith	4	14	14	14	4	Vehicle (Tank, Heavy, Skimmer)	1 Monolith

WARGEAR:
• **Four gauss flux arcs** (pg 113)
• **Particle whip** (pg 113)
• **Eternity gate** (pg 115)

SPECIAL RULES:
• **Deep Strike**
• **Living Metal** (pg 112)

ANNIHILATION BARGE

Annihilation Barges are the Necrons' favoured anti-infantry support platforms. At the Overlord's command, the Annihilation Barges' ancient repulsor sleds are coaxed back into life and the vehicles accompany the tomb world's army to war. Each is armed with a linked pair of tesla destructors – enormous energy cannons that fire arcs of crackling lightning and are death to lightly armoured targets. These heavy gun-platforms are seldom swift enough to keep pace with the advance of the army, however – instead, they are deployed as defences for strategic locations where their blistering firepower throws back all but the most determined infantry offensives. Many a hapless scout's last sight has been the bulky silhouette of an Annihilation Barge rising from cover, the ominous whine of its tesla destructors foretelling their demise.

	BS	F	S	R	HP	Unit Type	Unit Composition
		⌐Armour⌐					
Annihilation Barge	4	11	11	11	3	Vehicle (Skimmer, Open-topped)	1 Annihilation Barge

WARGEAR:
- **Gauss cannon** (pg 113)
- **Twin-linked tesla destructor** (pg 114)
- **Quantum shielding** (pg 115)

SPECIAL RULES:
- **Living Metal** (pg 112)

OPTIONS:
- May exchange gauss cannon for tesla cannon (pg 114) ....*free*

DOOMSDAY ARK

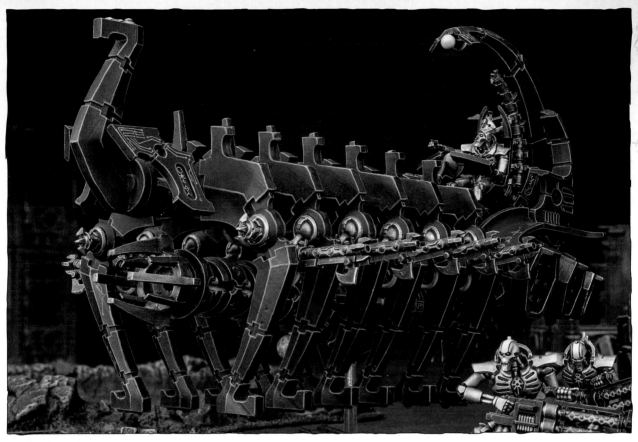

Victory through overwhelming firepower is a common tenet of Necron strategic thinking. Nowhere is this more evident than in the Doomsday Ark. Though deceptively fragile at first glance, the Doomsday Ark is a self-propelled energy cannon whose raw, unsubtle firepower is so vastly destructive that a single shot can turn the tide of a battle. Cradled in the ribcage-like chassis of the Ark, the cannon thrums and crackles with barely contained power, the ferocious energies trapped within its glowing coils capable of blasting virtually anything it is aimed at from existence. Rather than rely upon evasion or resilience, the Doomsday Ark's entire defensive strategy is the pre-emptive strike – after all, enemies are infinitely less threatening after being rendered into drifting clouds of their component atoms.

	BS	⌈Armour⌉ F	S	R	HP	Unit Type	Unit Composition
Doomsday Ark	4	11	11	11	4	Vehicle (Skimmer, Open-topped)	1 Doomsday Ark

WARGEAR:
- **Doomsday cannon** (pg 113)
- **Two gauss flayer arrays** (pg 113)
- **Quantum shielding** (pg 115)

SPECIAL RULES:
- **Living Metal** (pg 112)

TRANSCENDENT C'TAN

Transcendent C'tan are all that remain of the once mighty star-gods. They are echoes of their former selves, splinters of energy that survived the Necrons' betrayal and were trammelled in tesseract labyrinths. Ancient, archaic technologies shackle these beings to the will of their Necron masters, compelling them to obey and reducing them to the merest echoes of their ancient majesty. Yet even in their reduced and fettered state, Transcendent C'tan are still beings of immense power: they can manifest energy blasts, control the minds of lesser beings, manipulate the flow of time, and banish foes to alternate realities. For all this, the C'tan are unwilling slaves and often pervert their masters' wishes, slaying their foes by means which they see fit rather than to please their captors.

The only hope of defeating a C'tan is to breach its necrodermis – the living shell that cages its raging essence and binds it to the material plane. Should the necrodermis' integrity be compromised, the C'tan Shard implodes in a blinding pulse of energy, obliterating anything nearby.

	WS	BS	S	T	W	I	A	Ld	Sv	Unit Type	Unit Composition
Transcendent C'tan	5	5	8	7	5	4	4	10	4+	Monstrous Creature (Character)	1 Transcendent C'tan

WARGEAR:
• **Powers of the C'tan**
  (pg 117)

SPECIAL RULES:
• **Deep Strike**
• **Eternal Warrior**
• **Fearless**

Immune to Natural Law: When moving, this model can move over all other models and terrain freely, and automatically passes Dangerous Terrain tests. However, it cannot end its move on top of other models and can only end its move on top of impassable terrain if it is possible to actually place the model on top of it.

Necrodermis: This model has a 4+ invulnerable save. If it is ever reduced to 0 Wounds, before removing the model as a casualty, each nearby unit (friend or foe) suffers a Strength 4 AP1 hit for each model it has within D6" of this model.

Writhing Worldscape: All enemy units treat open ground within 6" of a Transcendent C'tan as difficult terrain.

TESSERACT VAULT

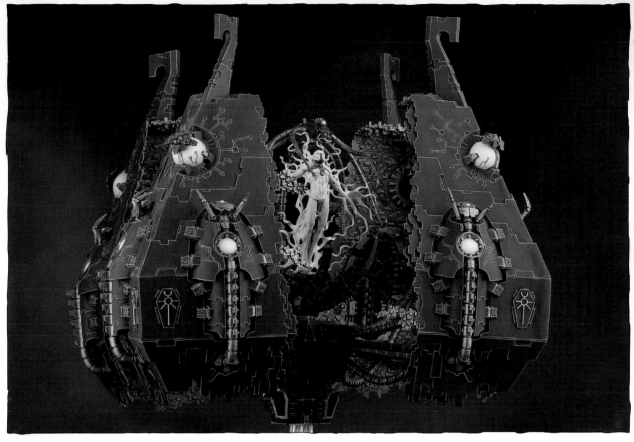

Only a race as ruthless and self-serving as the Necrons would think of unleashing a Tesseract Vault to further their aims – though each Vault is a potent weapon of war, the beings held within these floating prisons pose an almost incalculable threat. These Transcendent C'tan wield the coalescent power of so many shards that no mere tesseract labyrinth can hope to contain them – to allow such a being free rein is to invite destruction on a planetary scale. To counteract this threat, each Vault's hull contains layers of node matrices that draw power from the Transcendent C'tan itself, leeching the energies of the god-fragment to maintain the very cage that holds it. Yet even so muzzled, the Transcendent C'tan has might enough to scatter armies to the winds, pervert the flow of time and space, and drag stars from the heavens.

	BS	F	S	R	HP	Unit Type	Unit Composition
Tesseract Vault	4	14	14	14	9	Vehicle (Super-heavy Vehicle, Skimmer)	1 Tesseract Vault

WARGEAR:
• **Four tesla spheres** (pg 114)
• **Powers of the C'tan** (pg 117)

SPECIAL RULES:
• **Living Metal** (pg 112)

The Bound Coalescent:
When a Tesseract Vault uses Powers of the C'tan, measure line of sight and distance from the C'tan itself and resolve the attack at Ballistic Skill 5.

Vengeance of the Enchained: When a Tesseract Vault loses its last Hull Point, it always suffers a Titanic Explosion! – there is no need to roll on the Catastrophic Damage table.

OBELISK

The Obelisk hovers low over the battlefield, the somnolent hum of its gravitic repulsors sowing dread in the hearts of the foe. As it drifts into view, black lightning arcing across its glowing hull, the Obelisk presents a darkly majestic sight. Yet wonder turns swiftly to horror as the Obelisk's weapons cycle up, glowing tesla spheres irising open to spit crawling skeins of lightning that reduce those nearby to blackened, twitching husks. It is against enemy aircraft that the Obelisk proves most potent, for its primary function is to scour alien invasion craft from a tomb world's skies. To this end, the Obelisk's core contains a minute gravitic singularity – a howling rent in reality whose energies can be unleashed as a roiling gravimetric pulse to swat aircraft from the sky with arrogant ease.

	BS	F	S	R	HP	Unit Type	Unit Composition
		⌐Armour⌐					
Obelisk	4	14	14	14	6	Vehicle (Super-heavy Vehicle, Skimmer)	1 Obelisk

WARGEAR:
- **Four tesla spheres** (pg 114)

SPECIAL RULES:
- **Deep Strike**
- **Living Metal** (pg 112)

Gravity Pulse: All enemy Flyer, Skimmer, Jetbike and Flying Monstrous Creature units treat all terrain within 18" of an Obelisk, including open ground, as dangerous terrain. Zooming Flyers and Swooping Monstrous Creatures must also take a Dangerous Terrain test if they move within 18" of an Obelisk, even though they do not normally take dangerous terrain tests.

Sleeping Sentry: When you deploy an Obelisk, you can choose whether it is powered up or powered down. If it is powered up, it follows the normal rules for a vehicle of its type. If it is powered down, it may not move or shoot, but has a 3+ invulnerable save. You can choose to power up the Obelisk at the start of any of your Movement phases. An Obelisk that arrives by Deep Strike is automatically considered to be powered up. Once powered up, an Obelisk cannot power down later in the game.

IMOTEKH THE STORMLORD

PHAERON OF THE SAUTEKH DYNASTY

190 POINTS

Imotekh is the phaeron of the Sautekh Dynasty, an ever-expanding galactic empire that he rules with an iron fist. He is a supreme strategist – perhaps the most accomplished in the galaxy – and his military manoeuvres encompass entire star systems. Imotekh's plans are always many stages ahead of his foes', set to take advantage of their mistakes long before they are made. He designs counter-strategies and contingencies so that they trigger automatically, should certain circumstances occur or thresholds be crossed.

A master of using terror as a weapon, Imotekh leads his armies to war beneath the cover of billowing storm clouds that lash the foe with bolts of emerald lightning. Bloodswarm nanoscarabs spread confusion and horror amongst the enemy ranks, and draw in packs of ravening Flayed Ones to add to the carnage of his advance.

Imotekh has but one weakness – a compulsion to humble and disfigure his foes rather than slaying them outright. This dangerous conceit may yet prove the phaeron's downfall.

	WS	BS	S	T	W	I	A	Ld	Sv	Unit Type	Unit Composition
Imotekh the Stormlord	5	5	5	5	3	2	3	10	2+	Infantry (Character)	1 (Unique)

WARGEAR:
• **Gauntlet of fire** (pg 114)
• **Phase shifter** (pg 116)

WARLORD TRAIT:
• **Hyperlogical Strategist** (pg 112)

SPECIAL RULES:
• **Independent Character**
• **It Will Not Die**
• **Reanimation Protocols** (pg 112)

Lord of the Storm: If your army includes Imotekh the Stormlord, the Night Fighting special rule is always in effect during the first game turn (no dice roll is necessary). In addition, once per game, at the start of any friendly Shooting phase, roll a D6 for each enemy unit within 48" of Imotekh. On a 5+, that unit suffers D6 Strength 6 AP- hits. These hits are Randomly Allocated.

Bloodswarm Nanoscarabs: If your army includes Imotekh the Stormlord, friendly units of Flayed Ones can re-roll the scatter dice when arriving from Deep Strike Reserve.

ARTEFACT OF THE AEONS
Staff of the Destroyer: *This ancient and ornamental staff of light was originally wielded by Zehet, first ruler of the Sautekh, and has ever been a symbol of the dynasty's might. The bearer of the staff can unleash immolating beams of phase energy that ravage his target's form on all planes of existence.*

Range	S	AP	Type
18"	6	2	Assault 3

RECLAMATION LEGION

In the cold heart of every tomb world slumber tarnished metallic ranks of skull-faced Necron soldiers. These are the Reclamation Legions of the coreworlds, and it is from their number that the Overlords assemble their armies of conquest. When the Necrons march to war, the legion is the instrument of their wrath – ranks of lock-step Necron Warriors and towering Immortals in thrall to a single powerful Overlord. Tomb Blades range ahead of the army seeking out resistance, while the implacable advance of a Monolith anchors the legion and provides it with both heavy weapons support and a shimmering conduit back to the Necrons' tomb world. The sheer firepower of a single such force is more than enough to reduce an enemy army to ash – a task which the legion's warriors perform with a chilling, inexorable efficiency.

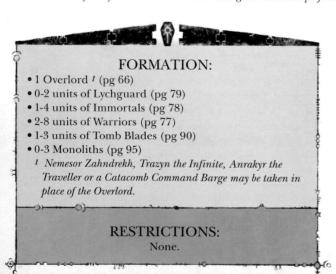

FORMATION:
- 1 Overlord ¹ (pg 66)
- 0-2 units of Lychguard (pg 79)
- 1-4 units of Immortals (pg 78)
- 2-8 units of Warriors (pg 77)
- 1-3 units of Tomb Blades (pg 90)
- 0-3 Monoliths (pg 95)
  ¹ Nemesor Zahndrekh, Trazyn the Infinite, Anrakyr the Traveller or a Catacomb Command Barge may be taken in place of the Overlord.

RESTRICTIONS:
None.

SPECIAL RULES:
- **Move Through Cover**
- **Relentless**

Enhanced Reanimation Protocols: You can re-roll Reanimation Protocols rolls of 1 for the Overlord from this Formation (or the model taken in place of the Overlord) and units from this Formation that are within 12" of him.

JUDICATOR BATTALION

The elite of the Necron armies, Triarch Praetorians hover above the battlefield upon gravity displacement packs, while in their shadow Triarch Stalkers incinerate enemies in incandescent storms of energy. It was the will of the Silent King that the dynasties reunite and the Necron Empire be restored, and it is to these Judicator Battalions that this auspicious task falls. Few Overlords or phaerons would be so foolish as to turn away the aid of the Praetorians, and so when the legions muster, any battalions in close proximity will join them in battle. However, these formations are not beholden to the commands of individual Overlords but fight for the Necron race as a whole; in doing such, they follow only the ancient edict of the Silent King himself.

FORMATION:
• 1 unit of Triarch Stalkers (pg 83)
• 2 units of Triarch Praetorians (pg 82)

RESTRICTIONS:
None.

SPECIAL RULES:
• **Move Through Cover**

Target Designated: At the start of each of the controlling player's Shooting phases, nominate one enemy unit within line of sight of a Triarch Stalker from this Formation. All units from this Formation can re-roll failed To Hit, To Wound and armour penetration rolls against the nominated unit until the end of the phase.

DESTROYER CULT

Life is a blight upon the galaxy that the Destroyers would see utterly extinguished. Even among the soulless ranks of the Necron dynasties, the Destroyer Cults are considered excessive in their hatred of the young races. A Destroyer Cult manifests when a Necron Lord steps upon the path of the Destroyer. His mind consumed with a repulsion for all life and a hatred of its weaknesses, the Destroyer Lord exists only to vent his cold fury upon his enemies. By instinct, other Destroyers will be drawn to the lord like rift-sharks lured from the shadows by the scent of blood. Driven into a killing fury by the massed presence of so many Destroyers, the cult will scour the battlefield of all life, leaving only smoking corpses in their wake.

FORMATION:
- 1 Destroyer Lord (pg 69)
- 3 units of Destroyers (pg 91)
- 0-1 units of Heavy Destroyers (pg 92)

RESTRICTIONS:
Each unit of Destroyers must consist of at least 3 models.

SPECIAL RULES:
- **Move Through Cover**

Fearsome Ruler: If this Formation is chosen as your Primary Detachment, you can re-roll the result when rolling on the Warlord Traits table in *Codex: Necrons*.

Extermination Protocols: All units in this Formation re-roll failed To Wound rolls and Armour Penetration rolls in the Shooting phase.

DEATHBRINGER FLIGHT

Cleaving across the sky like a screaming blade, formations of Doom Scythes herald the death of worlds. Those on the ground are subjected to twin horrors: the first is the blood-chilling wail emitted by the craft's motive drive, a sound that claws at the core of the primitive subconscious of mortal creatures and sends them scrambling for cover. The second – the Necron death ray – is a weapon so powerful that it turns anything it touches into atomic mist in mere seconds. When scrambled against large or high-priority enemies, the craft in a Deathbringer Flight can link their tactical subroutines into a single super-engram, locking their death rays onto a single target and obliterating it in a concentrated barrage of focused weapons fire.

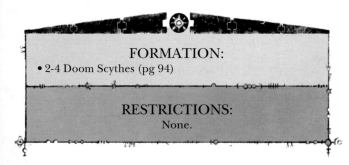

FORMATION:
• 2-4 Doom Scythes (pg 94)

RESTRICTIONS:
None.

SPECIAL RULES:

Amalgamated Targeting Data: When a Doom Scythe from this Formation fires its death ray at an enemy unit, add 2 to its Ballistic Skill for each other Doom Scythe from this Formation that has shot at the same enemy unit this turn.

Wailing Cacophony: All enemy units that are within 12" of at least two Doom Scythes from this Formation have -1 Leadership.

LIVING TOMB

Ghostly lights and spectral arcs of energy herald the arrival of a Necron invasion force – their foes look on in confusion, little knowing the terror about to be unleashed. Then, with an ear-splitting shriek, reality is torn asunder and a massive Obelisk flanked by Monoliths materialises in a storm of crackling energy. This is the Living Tomb – the nexus from which the legions will march forth to conquer the world. Enemies with the misfortune to be in the shadow of the Living Tomb when it arrives will be lashed with gauss fire, their very bodies scattered like embers from a dying fire. Moments later, eternity gates flicker to terrible life and the first skeletal shadows take shape within. Within minutes, the Living Tomb will be surrounded by the first legions, and the Necrons will have their foothold upon the planet.

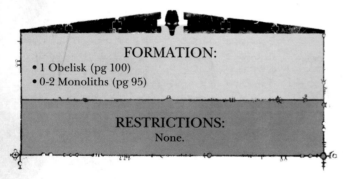

FORMATION:
- 1 Obelisk (pg 100)
- 0-2 Monoliths (pg 95)

RESTRICTIONS:
None.

SPECIAL RULES:

Precision Arrival: All units in this Formation must be placed into Deep Strike Reserve. Do not make Reserve Rolls for the Obelisk from this Formation; it automatically arrives on the controlling player's second turn. When arriving from Deep Strike Reserve, Monoliths from this Formation do not scatter if they are placed within 12" of the Obelisk from this Formation.

Tomb Nexus: Immediately after a Monolith from this Formation arrives from Deep Strike Reserve, you can choose one friendly unit with the Necrons Faction consisting entirely of models with either the Infantry or Jump Infantry unit type that is in Reserves or Ongoing Reserves. The chosen unit is placed as if it were disembarking from the Monolith's eternity gate. Any models that cannot be placed are removed as casualties, but the unit is otherwise treated exactly as if it were disembarking from a Transport vehicle.

Many phaerons have little patience for protracted sieges or wars of attrition, preferring instead to swiftly overwhelm their enemies with extreme levels of firepower. When a particularly stubborn foe has provoked the displeasure of the Overlord, he will summon forth an Annihilation Nexus, so the enemy might be suitably punished for their folly. Prized among the possessions of many Overlords are their Doomsday Arks and the rare dark energy cannons they carry into battle. Few things stir the cold emotions of a Necron noble like seeing his enemies erased from existence by the reality-rending blast of the Ark's cannon. Even so, such tools of obliteration are never risked in battle lightly, and thus the Arks of the Nexus are supported by twinned Annihilation Barges to see off lesser threats.

FORMATION:
- 1 Doomsday Ark (pg 97)
- 2 Annihilation Barges (pg 96)

RESTRICTIONS:
None.

SPECIAL RULES:
Quantum Deflection: If the Doomsday Ark from this Formation's quantum shielding is deactivated at the start of any of the controlling player's Movement phases, you can nominate an Annihilation Barge from this Formation within 6" that has active quantum shielding. That Annihilation Barge's quantum shielding is immediately deactivated, and the Doomsday Ark's quantum shielding is immediately reactivated.

CANOPTEK HARVEST

Floating, scuttling and ghosting through the blasted ruins of burning worlds, the Canoptek constructs harvest the living and the dead. Sometimes, an Overlord will gather together his robotic underlings and set them the specific task of scouring the battlefield for resources. Their mechanical minds slaved to the artificial intelligence of a Canoptek Spyder, the swarm of constructs becomes a harvest. Feeding on the fallen, the swarm converts mortal remains into energy for the Overlord, with little thought to whether or not the fallen try and resist. If the harvest is challenged, then the Canoptek Spyder reacts using a plethora of adaptive subroutines, allowing them to better focus on self-repair, speed or rendering down anything unfortunate enough to fall under their clicking metal mandibles.

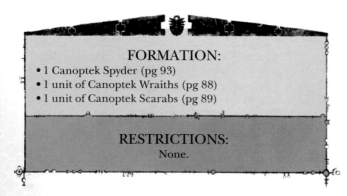

FORMATION:
• 1 Canoptek Spyder (pg 93)
• 1 unit of Canoptek Wraiths (pg 88)
• 1 unit of Canoptek Scarabs (pg 89)

RESTRICTIONS:
None.

SPECIAL RULES:
• Move Through Cover
• Relentless

Adaptive Subroutines: At the start of each of the controlling player's Movement phases, choose one of the following special rules: Fleet, Reanimation Protocols, Shred. The Canoptek Spyder from this Formation, and all units from this Formation within 12" of the Canoptek Spyder from this Formation, benefit from the effects of the chosen special rule until the start of the controlling player's next Movement phase.

ROYAL COURT

Like the blazing heart of a vast, ancient star system, a Necron Overlord is surrounded by a court of sworn Lords and loyal Crypteks. These are his trusted lieutenants, advisors and technomancers, each one having earned the right to bask in the terrible, radiant glory of their liege. Upon the field of war, the Royal Court becomes an extension of the will of the Overlord, executing his orders and driving his legions to victory against his foes. Of course, each court harbours those who would see their own star rise, perhaps even to eclipse the light of their master's, and so its Lords and Crypteks are always determined to prove their worth and thus advance their own agendas. For the Overlord, the court is not just a powerful tool of war, but also a means of keeping his potential rivals firmly under his burning scrutiny.

FORMATION:

- 1 Overlord *1* (pg 66)
- 1-3 Lords *2* (pg 67)
- 1-3 Crypteks *3* (pg 68)

1 Imotekh the Stormlord, Nemesor Zahndrekh, Trazyn the Infinite, Anrakyr the Traveller or a Catacomb Command Barge may be taken in place of the Overlord.

2 Vargard Obyron may be taken in place of a Lord.

3 Illuminor Szeras or Orikan the Diviner may be taken in place of a Cryptek.

RESTRICTIONS:

None.

SPECIAL RULES:
- **Move Through Cover**
- **Relentless**

Wisdom of the Aeons: If the Overlord from this Formation (or the model taken in place of the Overlord) is chosen as your Warlord, you can re-roll the result when rolling on the Warlord Traits table in *Codex: Necrons*.

APPENDIX

This section of the book details many of the rules for using an army of Necrons in your games of Warhammer 40,000, including their unique Warlord Traits, wargear and Tactical Objectives. The profiles page at the end provides a list of unit and weapons profiles for reference during your games.

NECRONS SPECIAL RULES

A Necron army uses a number of special rules that are common to several of its units, which are collected here for your convenience. Special rules that are unique to particular units are presented in the relevant unit entry instead. Other, more common rules are simply listed by name – these are all described in full in the Special Rules section of *Warhammer 40,000: The Rules*.

REANIMATION PROTOCOLS

Necrons have sophisticated self-repair systems that return even critically damaged warriors to the fight.

When a model with this special rule suffers an unsaved Wound, it can make a special Reanimation Protocols roll to avoid being wounded. This is not a saving throw and so can be used against attacks that state 'no saves of any kind are allowed'. Reanimation Protocols rolls may even be taken against hits with the Instant Death special rule, but cannot be used against hits from Destroyer weapons or any special rule or attack that states that the model is 'removed from play'.

Roll a D6 each time the model suffers an unsaved Wound, subtracting 1 from the result if the hit that inflicted the Wound had the Instant Death special rule. On a 5+, discount the unsaved Wound – treat it as having been saved. Certain special rules and wargear items can provide modifiers to this dice roll; these are cumulative, but the required dice roll can never be improved to be better than 4+.

If a unit has both the Reanimation Protocols and Feel No Pain special rules, you can choose to use one special rule or the other to attempt to avoid the Wound, but not both. Choose which of the two special rules you will use each time a model suffers an unsaved Wound.

LIVING METAL

Necron vehicles are composed of a semi-sentient alloy capable of incredible feats of resilience and auto-reconstitution.

A model with this special rule ignores the effects of Crew Shaken (but still loses a Hull Point). At the end of each of your turns, roll a D6 for each of your Heavy or Super-heavy vehicles with this special rule that has less than its starting number of Hull Points, but has not been destroyed. On a roll of a 6, that model regains a Hull Point lost earlier in the game.

WARLORD TRAITS

When generating Warlord traits for a Warlord with the Necrons Faction, you can either roll on one of the Warlord Traits tables in *Warhammer 40,000: The Rules* or roll on the table to the right.

WARLORD TRAITS TABLE

D6 WARLORD TRAIT

1 Enduring Will: *This Warlord is possessed of the iron resolve that has allowed the Necron race to cheat death and endure eternity. No mere mortal weaponry will prevent him from achieving his goals.*
Your Warlord has the Eternal Warrior special rule.

2 Eternal Madness: *This Warlord's sanity suffered more than most during the Great Sleep, but for all his ravings and strange commands, his every action is driven by a zealous conviction.*
Your Warlord has the Zealot special rule.

3 Immortal Hubris: *To this Necron noble, the lesser races of the galaxy are little better than crawling vermin, and he knows nothing but amused contempt for even the most fearsome of foes.*
Your Warlord and all friendly units with the Necrons Faction within 12" of him re-roll all failed Morale, Pinning and Fear tests.

4 Hyperlogical Strategist: *This Warlord can apply a filter of infallible logic to develop unbeatable strategies.*
Whilst your Warlord is alive, you may add or subtract 1 from any of your Reserves Rolls and rolls to Seize the Initiative (choose after each roll is made).

5 Implacable Conqueror: *This Warlord is a merciless foe, a conqueror of worlds who strides at the head of his legions and sweeps away all who stand before him.*
Your Warlord and all friendly units with the Necrons Faction within 12" of him have the Relentless and Crusader special rules.

6 Honourable Combatant: *A strict adherent to the ancient honour codes, this noble will countenance no action that contravenes them – be it from friend or foe.*
Your Warlord must always issue or accept a challenge if able to do so, and re-rolls all failed To Hit rolls when fighting in a challenge. No friendly character other than Vargard Obyron can attempt a Glorious Intervention in a challenge involving the Warlord. If an enemy refuses a challenge issued by the Warlord, the Warlord gains the Hatred special rule for the remainder of the game.

ARMOURY OF THE ANCIENTS

This section of *Codex: Necrons* lists the weapons and equipment used by the Necrons, along with the rules for using them in your games of Warhammer 40,000. Equipment that is carried by named characters is detailed in the appropriate entry in the datasheets (pg 64 to 109), while weapons and equipment used by all the other types of units are detailed here.

RANGED WEAPONS

DEATH RAY

A heavy, crystalline array that juts from the underside of each Doom Scythe, the death ray fires an irresistible beam of light that vaporises infantry and tanks alike.

Range	S	AP	Type
24"	10	1	Heavy 1, Blast, Lance

DOOMSDAY CANNON

Even fired at low power, the doomsday cannon is a fearsome weapon; when firing at full effect, nothing less than a Titan's void shields can offer hope of protection.

	Range	S	AP	Type
Low power	24"	8	3	Heavy 1, Blast
High power	72"	10	1	Primary Weapon 1, Large Blast, Divert Power

Divert Power: A vehicle can only fire a weapon with this rule if it remained stationary in its preceding Movement phase.

GAUSS WEAPONS

Gauss weapons vary in appearance from the rifle-sized flayers to the massive heavy gauss cannon. Unlike more conventional energy weapons, a gauss projector emits a molecular disassembling beam, reducing flesh, bone and even armour to its constituent atoms.

	Range	S	AP	Type
Gauss flayer	24"	4	5	Rapid Fire, Gauss
Gauss flayer array	24"	4	5	Salvo 5/10, Gauss, Independent Targeting
Gauss blaster	24"	5	4	Rapid Fire, Gauss
Gauss flux arc	24"	5	4	Heavy 3, Gauss, Independent Targeting
Gauss cannon	24"	5	3	Heavy 2, Gauss
Heavy gauss cannon	36"	9	2	Heavy 1, Gauss

Gauss: When firing a weapon with this special rule, a To Wound roll of a 6 wounds automatically, regardless of the target's Toughness. Against vehicles and buildings, an Armour Penetration roll of a 6 that does not cause a penetrating hit automatically causes a glancing hit.

Independent Targeting: A weapon with this special rule can fire at a different target to the vehicle's other weapons, but cannot target a unit forced to disembark as a result of a prior shooting attack made by the same vehicle during the same Shooting phase.

PARTICLE WEAPONS

These weapons emit a stream of minuscule antimatter particles that detonate upon contact with their target. They are incredibly reliable, needing only enough energy to maintain the containment field that prevents the anti-matter from detonating within the weapon's own firing mechanism.

	Range	S	AP	Type
Particle caster	12"	6	5	Pistol
Particle beamer	24"	6	5	Heavy 1, Blast
Particle shredder	24"	7	4	Heavy 1, Large Blast
Particle whip	24"	8	3	Ordnance 1, Large Blast

ROD OF COVENANT

The rod of covenant is a tool of swift execution for those found wanting by the Triarch Praetorians. Within the head of each weapon is caged a roiling fragment of a dying star bound within a potent force field, capable of burning through a foe's armour as if it were dry parchment. This energy can further be directed by the rod's wielder in a searing blast which, while short ranged, can reduce even a Necron to a smouldering pool of fused metal – organic creatures simply explode into clouds of flaming ash.

Range	S	AP	Type
12"	5	2	Assault 1
-	User	2	Melee, Two-handed

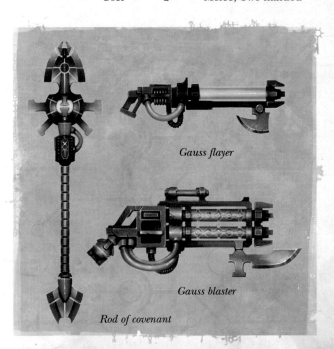

Gauss flayer

Gauss blaster

Rod of covenant

STAFF OF LIGHT

The staff of light is both a weapon and a symbol of authority. Its haft is actually a disguised power generator rod, and the crest a finely tuned focussing device, allowing the wielder to unleash crackling bolts of energy at his foes.

Range	S	AP	Type
12"	5	3	Assault 3

SYNAPTIC DISINTEGRATOR

This rifle fires a compressed leptonic beam that destroys synaptic tissue. Beginning within the target's brain and spreading in microseconds throughout their entire body, molecules unbond with one another, causing the luckless target to crumple limply to the ground like a puppet with its strings severed.

Range	S	AP	Type
24"	X	5	Rapid Fire, Sniper

TACHYON ARROW

The tachyon arrow is an intricate wrist-mounted energy caster. When activated, it transmutes a sliver of inert metal into an unstoppable thunderbolt capable of piercing the heart of a mountain, or instantly erasing a foe from existence.

Range	S	AP	Type
120"	10	1	Assault 1, One Use Only

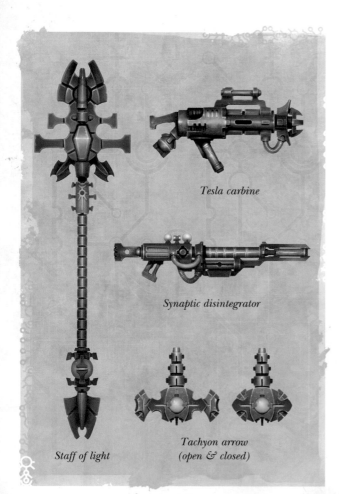

Staff of light

Tesla carbine

Synaptic disintegrator

Tachyon arrow (open & closed)

FLAMER WEAPONS

All of the following weapons are Flamer weapons for the purposes of any special rules that interact with Flamer weapons as described in *Warhammer 40,000: The Rules.*

GAUNTLET OF FIRE

The gauntlet of fire takes the form of an armoured glove and vambrace, whose length crackles and flows with green flame. The gauntlet's mechanisms are controlled by a series of submechadermal filaments, allowing the wielder a level of control over the gauntlet as fine as if it were his own hand.

Range	S	AP	Type
Template	4	5	Assault 1

HEAT RAY

The heat ray is a multipurpose fusion weapon whose focussed blasts can slice an enemy tank in half from end to end. Should the heat ray be turned upon enemy infantry, the operator can instead fire a dispersed beam, bathing his target in clouds of scorching plasma.

	Range	S	AP	Type
Dispersed	Template	5	4	Heavy 1
Focussed	24"	8	1	Heavy 2, Melta

TESLA WEAPONS

A tesla weapon unleashes a bolt of living lightning that crackles from foe to foe after hitting its target, charring flesh and melting armour. Tesla bolts feed off the energy released by the destruction, the lightning becoming more furious with every fresh arc.

	Range	S	AP	Type
Tesla carbine	24"	5	-	Assault 1, Tesla
Tesla cannon	24"	6	-	Heavy 2, Tesla
Tesla destructor	24"	7	-	Heavy 4, Tesla
Tesla sphere	24"	7	-	Heavy 5, Tesla

Tesla: When firing a weapon with this special rule, a To Hit roll of a 6 causes 2 additional hits on the target. Snap Shots never cause additional hits as a result of this special rule.

TRANSDIMENSIONAL BEAMER

This device was designed as a convenient method to dispose of unwanted debris, machinery and failed experiments in throw-away pocket dimensions. Yet it can just as easily be turned upon living foes, banishing them forever to the nether-realms.

Range	S	AP	Type
12"	4	2	Heavy 1, Exile Ray

Exile Ray: When firing a weapon with this special rule, a To Wound roll of a 6 wounds automatically, regardless of the target's Toughness, and the Wound has the Instant Death special rule. Against vehicles and buildings, an Armour Penetration roll of a 6 causes a penetrating hit, regardless of the target's Armour Value.

MELEE WEAPONS

FLAYER CLAW

Flayed Ones replace their hands with an array of lethally sharp blades, claws and mechanical shears to better tear and shred their prey into ribbons of bloody flesh.

Range	S	AP	Type
-	User	5	Melee, Shred

HYPERPHASE SWORD

The energy blade of a hyperphase sword vibrates across dimensional states, and can easily slice through armour and flesh to sever the vital organs within.

Range	S	AP	Type
-	User	3	Melee

ROD OF COVENANT

See page 113.

VOIDBLADE

The gleaming black edge of a voidblade flickers in and out of existence, causing the molecular bonds of any material it comes into contact with to instantaneously disintegrate.

Range	S	AP	Type
-	User	4	Melee, Entropic Strike, Rending

Entropic Strike: If a model has this special rule, or is attacking with a Melee weapon that has this special rule, a To Wound roll of a 6 wounds automatically, regardless of the target's Toughness. Against vehicles and buildings, an Armour Penetration roll of 6 that does not cause a penetrating hit automatically causes a glancing hit.

WARSCYTHE

Warscythes are energy-bladed battle staves, and have been the favoured weapons of Necron Lords and their bodyguards for many thousands of years. Heavy and cumbersome, in the hands of a lesser creature a warscythe would be of little threat, but when wielded by the tireless mechanical musculature of a Necron, it is a most formidable weapon.

Range	S	AP	Type
-	+2	2	Melee, Armourbane, Two-handed

WHIP COILS

Some Canoptek Wraiths are equipped with writhing mechanical tendrils that whip around at high speeds, splitting flesh and flensing their prey in an eye-blink.

Range	S	AP	Type
-	User	-	Melee, Swiftstrike

Swiftstrike: A model attacking with this weapon adds 3 to its Initiative during the Fight sub-phase.

Hyperphase sword

Voidblade

Warscythe

NECRON VEHICLE EQUIPMENT

ETERNITY GATE

A Monolith's eternity gate is a dimensional corridor between the battlefield and a tomb world, allowing legions of Necron warriors to cross vast distances and enter the fray with a single step.

At the start of each friendly turn, you may choose one friendly unit with the Necrons Faction consisting entirely of models with either the Infantry or Jump Infantry unit type that is in Reserves, Ongoing Reserves, or is on the table and not locked in combat. If the chosen unit is in Reserves or Ongoing Reserves, it automatically arrives this turn (no dice roll is required) and it is placed as if it were disembarking from the Monolith's portal at the start of the Movement phase. If the chosen unit is currently on the battlefield, it is first removed from the table and then placed as described above. Any models that cannot be placed are removed as casualties, but the unit is otherwise treated exactly as if it were disembarking from a Transport vehicle.

QUANTUM SHIELDING

Necron quantum shielding is a marvel of science, existing only at the precise moment of deflection – at all other times there is no indication of its presence. They are, however, temperamental devices, prone to malfunction if overloaded.

A vehicle equipped with active quantum shielding counts all of its Front and Side Armour Values as 13. A vehicle's quantum shielding is active until it suffers a penetrating hit, at which point it immediately deactivates. For the remainder of the battle after a vehicle's quantum shielding deactivates, all subsequent hits against that vehicle (including hits made from subsequent shooting attacks in the same phase – either from a different weapon or a different unit – or hits made at a lower Initiative step in close combat) are treated as though the vehicle was not equipped with quantum shielding.

TECHNOARCANA

CHRONOMETRON

These eye-shaped devices project a bubble of energy that can alter the flow of time itself, slowing incoming projectiles such that those nearby can simply move out of their path.

A model with a chronometron and his unit have a 5+ invulnerable save against all Shooting attacks.

DISPERSION SHIELD

The force barrier projected by a dispersion shield can be used to fend off close combat attacks or deflect incoming enemy fire.

A model equipped with a dispersion shield has a 3+ invulnerable save. However, it can never claim the Two Weapons bonus in the Fight sub-phase.

FABRICATOR CLAW ARRAY

This clicking, whirring proliferation of energy tools is primarily intended for maintenance and repair.

In each of your Shooting phases, instead of firing a weapon, a model with a fabricator claw array can choose to repair a single friendly vehicle that it is in base contact with. To repair a vehicle, roll a D6. If the result is a 4 or more, you may either restore a Hull Point lost earlier in the battle or repair a Weapon Destroyed or Immobilised result suffered earlier in the battle; this is effective immediately.

GLOOM PRISM

The gloom prism's energy field creates a zone shrouded from Warp-spawned powers.

A model equipped with a gloom prism and all friendly units within 12" have the Adamantium Will special rule.

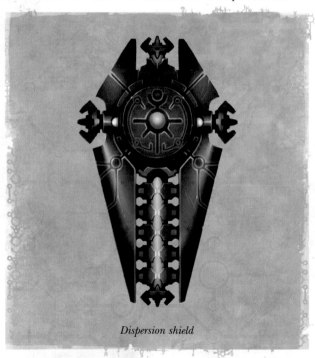

Dispersion shield

MINDSHACKLE SCARABS

At the bearer's command, tiny mindshackle scarabs burrow into their target's brain, bypassing cerebral functions and robbing the unfortunate victim of their wits.

When fighting in a challenge, a model with mindshackle scarabs has the Fear special rule. Fear tests taken as a result of mindshackle scarabs must be taken on 3D6.

NEBULOSCOPE

This arcane device allows the Tomb Blade's pilot to track his prey through different dimensions, leaving them no place to hide.

If a model is equipped with a nebuloscope, all of its ranged weapons have the Ignores Cover special rule.

PHASE SHIFTER

A phase shifter causes its bearer to fluctuate in and out of an incorporeal state. Blows aimed at the bearer pass through nothing but empty air.

A phase shifter confers a 4+ invulnerable save. If the bearer is the rider of a Chariot, then only the rider benefits from this invulnerable save.

PHYLACTERY

This scarab-shaped charm is a powerful self-repair device, filled with tiny, spider-like creations that swarm over the bearer's wounds, rapidly knitting them together with living metal fibres.

A model equipped with a phylactery has the It Will Not Die special rule. If the model is the rider of a Chariot, both he and the Chariot have the It Will Not Die special rule.

RESURRECTION ORB

This glowing sphere focuses energy into the regeneration circuits of nearby Necrons, enhancing their ability to self-repair.

A resurrection orb can be activated once per game, immediately after an unsuccessful Reanimation Protocols roll has been made for the bearer of the resurrection orb or another model in the same unit. You can re-roll the failed Reanimation Protocols roll, and any further failed Reanimation Protocols rolls made for the bearer or any other model in the same unit, until the end of the phase.

SHADOWLOOM

This generator projects an aura of unnatural darkness about the Tomb Blade, making it difficult to track and target.

A model equipped with a shadowloom has +1 cover save. If it does not already have a cover save, it instead gains a 6+ cover save.

SHIELD VANES

Tomb Blades that are deployed directly into the midst of a world's defences are often equipped with additional armour panels.

Shield vanes confer a 3+ Armour Save.

POWERS OF THE C'TAN

To the Shards of the C'tan, reality is merely another weapon to turn upon their foes. It is within the prodigious power of these god-fragments to summon forth storms of annihilating negative matter, shatter the very bones of a planet itself or even cast their enemies out of existence with but a thought.

Models armed with Powers of the C'tan can use them as a ranged weapon in the Shooting phase of their own turn. They cannot use them to fire Overwatch. Each time a model uses Powers of the C'tan, choose a target as normal then roll one D6 and consult the following table to determine which power is used.

1	Antimatter Meteor
2	Cosmic Fire
3	Seismic Assault
4	Sky of Falling Stars
5	Time's Arrow
6	Transdimensional Thunderbolt

Each of the Powers of the C'tan has two separate weapon profiles. When the C'tan Shard of the Nightbringer, the C'tan Shard of the Deceiver or a Transcendent C'tan uses one of these powers, use the Transcendent weapon profile; when a Tesseract Vault uses one of these powers, use the Coalescent weapon profile.

ANTIMATTER METEOR

The C'tan Shard gathers an orb of roiling antimatter, before hurling the crackling projectile into the midst of the foe.

	Range	S	AP	Type
Transcendent	24"	8	3	Assault 1, Large Blast
Coalescent	48"	8	3	Assault 1, Apocalyptic Blast

COSMIC FIRE

At the C'tan Shard's gestured command, a pillar of black fire streaks down from the heavens.

Cosmic Fire is a Flamer weapon for the purposes of any special rules that interact with Flamer weapons, as described in *Warhammer 40,000: The Rules*.

	Range	S	AP	Type
Transcendent	24"	6	4	Assault 1, Large Blast, Ignores Cover
Coalescent	48"	6	4	Assault 1, Apocalyptic Blast, Ignores Cover

SEISMIC ASSAULT

Stone fractures and ores flash burn into silvered steam as the C'tan Shard drags up tides of magma from deep below.

	Range	S	AP	Type
Transcendent	24"	6	4	Assault 10, Strikedown
Coalescent	48"	6	4	Assault 20, Strikedown

SKY OF FALLING STARS

Savagely beautiful orbs of coruscating light plummet from the cold depths of space, growing to roaring bale-stars as they approach.

	Range	S	AP	Type
Transcendent	24"	7	4	Assault 3, Large Blast, Barrage
Coalescent	48"	7	4	Assault 6, Apocalyptic Barrage

TIME'S ARROW

Mutating the flow of causality and remoulding the temporal stream, the C'tan erases its foe's very existence from space and time.

	Range	S	AP	Type
Transcendent	24"	D	1	Assault 1, Precision Shots
Coalescent	48"	D	1	Assault 2, Precision Shots

TRANSDIMENSIONAL THUNDERBOLT

The C'tan Shard projects a crackling bolt of energy from its outstretched palm, blasting its foe into oblivion.

	Range	S	AP	Type
Transcendent	24"	9	1	Assault 1, Tesla
Coalescent	48"	9	1	Assault 2, Tesla

Tesla: When firing a weapon with this special rule, a To Hit roll of a 6 causes 2 additional hits on the target. Snap Shots never cause additional hits as a result of this special rule.

ARTEFACTS OF THE AEONS

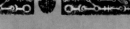

Artefacts of the Aeons are items of terrifying power, and each is older than many of the lesser races themselves. Only one of each of the following relics may be chosen per army.

THE GAUNTLET OF THE CONFLAGRATOR

Crafted by the Cryptek Harri'apt the Conflagrator, this gauntlet uses interdimensional energy-exchangers to open a microscopic conduit to the raging heart of a star. The superheated plasmic flame that erupts through this hole is forced down a cone of hyperdense gravitons that spew the energy forth in a blazing split-second cloud of unstoppable fury.

Range	S	AP	Type
Template	7	2	Assault 1, One Use Only

The Gauntlet of the Conflagrator is a Flamer weapon for the purposes of any special rules that interact with Flamer weapons as described in *Warhammer 40,000: The Rules*.

THE NIGHTMARE SHROUD

This heavy cloak of living-metal scales was forged by Ut-Hekneth the Unsleeping during his million-year madness. The cloak itself is virtually indestructible, each scale formed from quantum-folded layers of void-hardened adamantium bonded with a hyper-flexible energy weave. This is a by-product of its primary design however, which is to project the worst excesses of Ut-Hekneth's madness, assailing nearby enemies with phantasms of dread as potent as any mortal danger.

The Nightmare Shroud confers a 2+ Armour Save and the Fear special rule. In addition, once per game, during any friendly Shooting phase, the bearer can choose one enemy unit within 18". That unit must immediately take a Morale check (units with the Fearless or And They Shall Know No Fear special rule automatically pass this test).

THE ORB OF ETERNITY

The Orb of Eternity is thought to be the first resurrection orb ever created. For millennia, it rested in a primitive fane on the world of Ormandus, where the indigenous populace marvelled at its seemingly divine ability to effect repairs upon their technologies. Ever since this state of affairs was righted by a host of Triarch Praetorians, the orb is imparted as a boon to those nobles who are deemed worthy of such incredible power.

The Orb of Eternity can be activated once per game, immediately after an unsuccessful Reanimation Protocols roll has been made for the bearer of the Orb of Eternity or another model in the same unit. You can re-roll the failed Reanimation Protocols roll, and any further failed Reanimation Protocols rolls made for the bearer or any other model in the same unit, until the end of the phase. Furthermore, when the Orb of Eternity is activated, all Reanimation Protocols rolls made for the bearer or any other model in the same unit receive a +1 bonus until the end of the phase, including re-rolled Reanimation Protocols rolls.

THE SOLAR STAFF

The Solar Staff burns with the light of truth and honour, and when its powers are unleashed they are a bane to all shadows. Set loose, the staff's energies blaze outward in a mighty flare, as though a new sun was born. The darkness is driven back by this false dawn, and the foe reels as their eyes are blinded and their deceptions are laid bare.

Range	S	AP	Type
12"	5	3	Assault 3, Blind, Solar Pulse

Solar Pulse: Once per game, at the start of any turn, the bearer can use this special rule. When he does, the Night Fighting rules are not in effect for the remainder of the turn (if they were in effect). In addition, when this special rule is used, enemy units targeting the bearer or his unit can only fire Snap Shots until the start of the bearer's next turn.

THE VEIL OF DARKNESS

This device was fashioned from transpositanium, a substance so rare that it can only be found in a handful of places in the galaxy. It is highly sought after by the Necrons, and wars have been waged to secure it. Activated with a thought, the veil causes space and time to warp around its user and those near him, enfolding them in a swirling darkness. As the darkness fades, the user and his comrades appear elsewhere on the battlefield, transported through a miracle of arcane science.

The bearer of the Veil of Darkness has the Deep Strike special rule. In addition, once per game, at the start of any friendly Movement phase, the bearer can use the Veil of Darkness to remove himself and his unit from the table, even if they are locked in combat. They then immediately arrive anywhere on the board using the rules for Deep Strike.

VOIDREAPER

Legend has it that on the day Aza'gorod the Nightbringer was sundered into shards, this warscythe appeared in the armoury of the Nekthyst Dynasty's crownworld. Its blade is a sliver of the void; when swung, it cuts through more than just mere physical forms. Its victims drop to the ground as husks, their souls torn from their bodies like tattered shrouds before dissipating with final screams of horror.

Range	S	AP	Type
-	+2	2	Melee, Armourbane, Fleshbane, Master-crafted, Two-handed

TACTICAL OBJECTIVES

Codex: Necrons describes six Tactical Objectives to use in your games of Warhammer 40,000 that are exclusive to Necron players, and help to reflect their methodical and unrelenting method of war.

If your Warlord has the Necrons Faction, these Tactical Objectives replace the Capture & Control Tactical Objectives (numbers 11-16) described in *Warhammer 40,000: The Rules*.

If a Warhammer 40,000 mission has the Tactical Objectives special rule, players use the normal rules for using Tactical Objectives with the following exception: when a Necron player generates a Capture & Control objective (numbers 11, 12, 13, 14, 15 or 16), generate the corresponding Necrons Tactical Objective instead, as shown in the table opposite. Other Tactical Objectives (numbers 21-66) are generated normally.

D66	RESULT
11	Thrall of the Silent King
12	Dust and Ashes
13	Reclaim and Recapture
14	Age of the Machine
15	Slaughter the Living
16	Code of Combat

---

11 THRALL OF THE SILENT KING
TYPE: NECRONS
Knowingly or otherwise, you pursue some veiled agenda of the Silent King. You must strive furiously for its completion, for to do so is at the very core of your being.
When this Tactical Objective is generated, immediately generate a bonus Tactical Objective – this does not count towards the number of Active Tactical Objectives you currently have in play. If your Warlord or his unit achieves the bonus Tactical Objective, you score both the number of Victory Points stated on the bonus Tactical Objective and an additional D3 Victory Points. If this Tactical Objective is discarded, so too is the bonus Tactical Objective (and vice versa).

12 DUST AND ASHES
TYPE: NECRONS
The Necrons have seen civilisations rise and fall and the stars burn themselves black. Some enemies only need to be outlived to be ultimately defeated.
When this Tactical Objective is generated, nominate one of your characters with the Necrons Faction. Score 1 Victory Point at the end of the game if this character is still alive. Characters that are not on the table or are Falling Back at the end of the game count as destroyed for purposes of this Tactical Objective.

13 RECLAIM AND RECAPTURE
TYPE: NECRONS
Using hyperbinaric logic, key strategic targets have been identified across the battlefield. Your legions must reclaim them if tactical superiority is to be achieved.
Roll a D6 when this Tactical Objective is generated. If the result is an odd number, score D3 Victory points at the end of your turn if you control all 3 odd-numbered Objective Markers. If the result is an even number, score D3 Victory points at the end of your turn if you control all 3 even-numbered Objective Markers.

14 AGE OF THE MACHINE
TYPE: NECRONS
The crude war machines of the lesser races are an affront to the technological supremacy of the Necrons. Exterminate them.
Score 1 Victory Point at the end of your turn if at least one gun emplacement, enemy vehicle or enemy building was destroyed during your turn. If at least 3 gun emplacements, enemy vehicles or enemy buildings were destroyed during your turn, score D3 Victory Points instead. If any of the destroyed vehicles was a Super-heavy vehicle, or if any of the destroyed buildings had the Mighty Bulwark special rule, score an additional 3 Victory Points.

15 SLAUGHTER THE LIVING
TYPE: NECRONS
The young races cling to their primitive bodies of flesh and blood. Slaughter them like the animals they are; reduce their corpses to their constituent atoms.
Score 1 Victory Point at the end of your turn if at least one enemy unit was completely destroyed during your turn.

16 CODE OF COMBAT
TYPE: NECRONS
Though the civilisations of today are little more than barbarians, the ancient codes of honourable combat must still be upheld.
Score 1 Victory Point at the end of your turn if you issued at least one challenge during your turn.

DESIGNER'S NOTE – TACTICAL OBJECTIVES CARD DECK
If you own a deck of Necron Tactical Objective Cards, you can generate your Tactical Objectives by shuffling the deck and drawing the top card instead of rolling a D66. These should be kept face up, so your opponent can see which Tactical Objectives you have generated, unless the mission you are playing instructs you otherwise.

PROFILES

HQ

	WS	BS	S	T	W	I	A	Ld	Sv	Unit Type	Pg
Anrakyr the Traveller	5	5	5	5	3	2	3	10	3+	In (ch)	74
Cryptek	4	4	4	4	2	2	1	10	4+	In (ch)	68
Destroyer Lord	4	4	5	6	3	2	3	10	3+	In, Jp (ch)	69
Illuminor Szeras	4	4	4	4	2	2	4	10	3+	In (ch)	70
Lord	4	4	4	5	2	2	2	10	3+	In (ch)	67
Nemesor Zahndrekh	5	5	5	5	3	2	3	10	2+	In (ch)	70
Orikan the Diviner	4	4	4	4	2	2	2	10	4+	In (ch)	73
Orikan Empowered	5	5	7	7	4	4	4	10	4+	In (ch)	73
Overlord	5	5	5	5	3	2	3	10	3+	In (ch)	66
Trazyn the Infinite	5	5	5	5	3	2	3	10	3+	In (ch)	75
Vargard Obyron	6	4	5	5	2	2	3	10	2+	In (ch)	71

TROOPS

	WS	BS	S	T	W	I	A	Ld	Sv	Unit Type	Pg
Necron Warrior	4	4	4	4	1	2	1	10	4+	In	77
Immortal	4	4	4	4	1	2	1	10	3+	In	78

ELITES

	WS	BS	S	T	W	I	A	Ld	Sv	Unit Type	Pg
Deathmark	4	4	4	4	1	2	1	10	3+	In	80
Flayed One	4	1	4	4	1	2	3	10	4+	In	81
Lychguard	4	4	5	5	1	2	2	10	3+	In	79
C'tan Shard of the Deceiver	5	5	7	7	4	4	4	10	4+	MC (ch)	85
C'tan Shard of the Nightbringer	6	4	7	7	4	4	4	10	4+	MC (ch)	84
Triarch Praetorian	4	4	5	5	1	2	2	10	3+	In, J	82

FAST ATTACK

	WS	BS	S	T	W	I	A	Ld	Sv	Unit Type	Pg
Canoptek Wraith	4	4	6	5	2	2	3	10	3+	Be	88
Canoptek Scarab	2	2	3	3	3	2	4	10	6+	Be	89
Destroyer	4	4	4	5	2	2	1	10	3+	In, Jp	91
Heavy Destroyer	4	4	4	5	2	2	1	10	3+	In, Jp	91
Tomb Blade	4	4	4	5	1	2	1	10	4+	Jb	90

HEAVY SUPPORT

	WS	BS	S	T	W	I	A	Ld	Sv	Unit Type	Pg
Canoptek Spyder	3	3	6	6	3	2	2	10	3+	MC	93
Heavy Destroyer	4	4	4	5	2	2	1	10	3+	In, Jp	92
Transcendent C'tan	5	5	8	7	5	4	4	10	4+	MC (ch)	98

VEHICLES

	WS	BS	S	F	S	R	I	A	HP	Unit Type	Pg
Annihilation Barge	-	4	-	11	11	11	-	-	3	S, O	96
Catacomb Command Barge	-	4	-	11	11	11	-	-	3	Ct, S, F, O (ch)	76
Doom Scythe	-	4	-	11	11	11	-	-	3	Fl	94
Doomsday Ark	-	4	-	11	11	11	-	-	4	S, O	97
Ghost Ark	-	4	-	11	11	11	-	-	4	S, O, T	87
Monolith	-	4	-	14	14	14	-	-	4	Tk, Hv, S	95
Night Scythe	-	4	-	11	11	11	-	-	3	Fl, T	86
Obelisk	-	4	-	14	14	14	-	-	6	ShV, S	100
Triarch Stalker	4	4	7	11	11	11	2	3	3	W, O	83
Tesseract Vault	-	4	-	14	14	14	-	-	9	ShV, S	99

LORDS OF WAR

	WS	BS	S	T	W	I	A	Ld	Sv	Unit Type	Pg
Imotekh the Stormlord	5	5	5	5	3	2	3	10	2+	In (ch)	101

UNIT TYPES

Beasts = Be, *Chariot* = Ct, *Fast* = F, *Flyer* = Fl, *Heavy* = Hv, *Infantry* = In, *Jet Pack unit* = Jp, *Jetbike* = Jb, *Jump unit* = J, *Monstrous Creature* = MC, *Open-topped* = O, *Super-heavy Vehicle* = ShV, *Skimmer* = S, *Tank* = Tk, *Transport* = T, *Walker* = W, *Character* = (ch)

RANGED WEAPONS

Weapon	Range	S	AP	Type
Death ray	24"	10	1	Heavy 1, Blast, Lance
Doomsday cannon				
Low power	24"	8	3	Heavy 1, Blast
High power	72"	10	1	Primary Weapon 1, Large Blast, Divert Power
Gauntlet of fire	Template	4	5	Assault 1
Gauss blaster	24"	5	4	Rapid Fire, Gauss
Gauss cannon	24"	5	3	Heavy 2, Gauss
Gauss flayer	24"	4	5	Rapid Fire, Gauss
Gauss flayer array	24"	4	5	Salvo 5/10, Gauss, Independent Targeting
Gauss flux arc	24"	5	4	Heavy 3, Gauss, Independent Targeting
Heat ray				
Dispersed	Template	5	4	Heavy 1
Focussed	24"	8	1	Heavy 2, Melta
Heavy gauss cannon	36"	9	2	Heavy 1, Gauss
Particle beamer	24"	6	5	Heavy 1, Blast
Particle caster	12"	6	5	Pistol
Particle shredder	24"	7	4	Heavy 1, Large Blast
Particle whip	24"	8	3	Ordnance 1, Large Blast
Rod of covenant	12"	5	2	Assault 1
Staff of light	12"	5	3	Assault 3
Synaptic disintegrator	24"	X	5	Rapid Fire, Sniper
Tachyon arrow	120"	10	1	Assault 1, One Use Only
Tesla cannon	24"	6	-	Heavy 2, Tesla
Tesla carbine	24"	5	-	Assault 1, Tesla
Tesla destructor	24"	7	-	Heavy 4, Tesla
Tesla sphere	24"	7	-	Heavy 5, Tesla
Transdimensional beamer	12"	4	2	Heavy 1, Exile Ray

MELEE WEAPONS

Weapon	Range	S	AP	Type
Flayer claw	-	User	5	Melee, Shred
Hyperphase sword	-	User	3	Melee
Rod of covenant	-	User	2	Melee, Two-handed
Voidblade	-	User	4	Melee, Entropic Strike, Rending
Warscythe	-	+2	2	Melee, Armourbane, Two-handed
Whip coils	-	User	-	Melee, Swiftstrike

POWERS OF THE C'TAN

Weapon	Range	S	AP	Type
Antimatter Meteor				
Transcendent	24"	8	3	Assault 1, Large Blast
Coalescent	48"	8	3	Assault 1, Apocalyptic Blast
Cosmic Fire				
Transcendent	24"	6	4	Assault 1, Ignores Cover, Large Blast
Coalescent	48"	6	4	Assault 1, Ignores Cover Apocalyptic Blast
Seismic Assault				
Transcendent	24"	6	4	Assault 10, Strikedown
Coalescent	48"	6	4	Assault 20, Strikedown
Sky of Falling Stars				
Transcendent	24"	7	4	Assault 3, Large Blast, Barrage
Coalescent	48"	7	4	Assault 6, Apocalyptic Barrage
Time's Arrow				
Transcendent	24"	D	1	Assault 1, Precision Shots
Coalescent	48"	D	1	Assault 2, Precision Shots
Transdimensional Thunderbolt				
Transcendent	24"	9	1	Assault 1, Tesla
Coalescent	48"	9	1	Assault 2, Tesla